PHONOLOGICAL SKILLS
AND LEARNING TO READ

Phonological Skills and Learning to Read

Usha Goswami
Department of Experimental Psychology
University of Cambridge, U.K.

Peter Bryant
Department of Experimental Psychology
University of Oxford, U.K.

Lawrence Erlbaum Associates Ltd., Publishers
27 Palmeira Mansions
Church Road
Hove
East Sussex, BN3 2FA
U.K.

British Library Cataloguing in Publication Data
Goswami, Usha C.
   Phonological skills and learning to read. - (Essays in developmental psychology series).
   1. Children. reading skills. Development. Psychological aspects
   I. Title II. Bryant, Peter, *1937-* III. Series
   428.43019

   ISBN 0-86377-150-5
   ISBN 0-86377-151-3 pbk
   ISSN 0959-3977
Printed and bound in the United Kingdom by BPCC Wheatons, Exeter

Contents

Preface

When Erlbaum decided to launch its new series, *Essays in Developmental Psychology*, we immediately thought of a book on the relationship between children's phonological skills and their reading. It seems to us that the work on this subject is a good example of developmental psychology at its best. Experiments on the connection between children's awareness of sounds and the progress that they make in reading and spelling have been ingenious and remarkably successful. They have produced results of real practical significance, and at the same time raise issues, such as how to establish causal relationships in development, which have general significance in developmental psychology.

We want to establish that the connection exists, but our aim is to do more than that. In the past, people have tended to concentrate on the way that children learn how to link phonemes with single letters (grapheme-phoneme relations). Children certainly do learn to use grapheme-phoneme relations, but it is now clear that at a very early stage in reading they make other connections as well. They learn about sequences of letters and they connect these with sounds that contain two or more phonemes. We shall argue that their ability to make this sort of connection is based on their early experience with rhyming words.

We have been helped, more than we can say, in our thoughts on these issues by our colleagues in the Department of Experimental Psychology at Oxford. We are particularly grateful to Lynette Bradley, Ruth Campbell, Yuko Kimura, Clare Kirtley, Morag Maclean and Lucia Rego. We should like to thank Liz Darley and Cheng Chan for helping with the figures, and Betty Hammond for helping us to type the references. Uta Frith, Charles Hulme, Masao Takahashi and Geoff Underwood read a first draft of this manuscript and provided many helpful comments. We are grateful too to Merton College, Oxford for the Junior Research Fellowship which Usha Goswami held at the college while this book was being written. We also remember the children, head teachers and teachers of the many schools in and around Oxford who have cheerfully taken part in much of the research mentioned in this book. We owe them a special debt of thanks.

Usha Goswami and Peter Bryant
Oxford, December, 1989

CHAPTER 1

Phonological Awareness and Reading

WHAT IS PHONOLOGICAL AWARENESS?

Virtually any three or four year old child understands a simple, spoken word like "cat", but if you ask her about the sounds in that word she will be hard put to it to answer your question. Most children of this age would not be able to tell you what the word's middle sound is, for example, or how the word ends. When children learn to talk, their interest naturally is in the meaning of the words that they speak and hear. The fact that these words can be analysed in a different way—that each word consists of a unique sequence of identifiable sounds—is of little importance to them. They want to know the meaning of what someone else is saying, and they need be no more concerned with the actual sounds that make up each word when they listen to someone speaking than they are with the exact composition of the food that they eat each day.

In a year or so, however, these children have to learn to read and write words as well as to speak them, and that may mean that the component sounds in these words take on a new significance. Alphabetic letters represent sounds, and strings of letters, by representing a sequence of sounds, can signify spoken words. The letters "c" "a" "t" represent sounds which roughly add up to the word "cat". So, a child who is being taught to read English, German, Portuguese or any other alphabetic script may have to pay a great deal of attention to a word's sounds.

But it need not be so. The fact that individual alphabetic letters represent sounds does not necessarily mean that children learn to read words like "cat" by working out the individual sounds represented by each letter and then putting these sounds together. The child may, to take just one other possibility, recognise the word as a visual pattern without paying a great deal of attention to the individual letters or to the sounds that they represent.

We cannot assume, therefore, that children's awareness of sounds—or "phonological awareness", as it is often called—plays an important part when they learn to read and write. We have to establish by empirical means whether this connection exists or not and what form it takes. We need to discover if children are helped, and perhaps hindered sometimes, by their sensitivity to the constituent sounds in words.

One useful starting point in this quest is to recognise that "phonological awareness" is itself a blanket term. There may well be different forms of this kind of awareness, because there are different ways in which words and syllables can be divided up into smaller units of sound.

PHONEMES AND OTHER SPEECH UNITS

There are at least three ways of breaking up a word into its constituent sounds, and thus at least three possible forms of phonological awareness. Figure 1.1 shows what these are.

Syllables.   The first and perhaps the most obvious way is to break it up into its syllables. This poses very little difficulty for most children (Liberman, Shankweiler, Fischer & Carter, 1974). However, many words and particularly words which children first learn to read, are monosyllabic, and so awareness of syllables cannot be relevant to the constituent sounds of these words. We need to think of smaller units than the syllable.

Phonemes.   The second way does involve much smaller phonological segments. It is to divide words into phonemes. A phoneme is the smallest unit of sound that can change the meaning of a word. "Cat" and "mat" sound different and have different meanings because they differ in terms of one phoneme. Alphabetic letters typically represent phonemes, and thus strings of alphabetic letters represent sequences of phonemes. In order to see that a sequence of letters adds up to a meaningful word because it represents all the phonemes in that word, the child has to understand how that word is in effect a collection of phonemes.

The importance to the child of learning how to use the relationships between single letters and single phonemes, or "grapheme-phoneme" correspondences as these relationships are often called, has been widely recognised. Indeed, some people

	Syllable	Onset and rime	Phoneme
"cat"	cat	c - at	c -a -t
"string"	string	str - ing	s-t-r-i-n-g
"wigwam"	wig-wam	w- ig- w- am	w-i-g-w-a-m

FIG. 1.1.   Three ways to divide words into component sounds.

concerned with phonological awareness and its relation to children's success in learning to read have stopped here. In their view, awareness of phonemes plays a crucial role in learning to read and no other form of phonological awareness has much significance.

Intra-syllabic Units—Onset and Rime.

Yet there is a third and intermediate kind of phonological awareness and we ought to consider whether it too has any part to play in children's reading. Words can also be divided up into units that are larger than the single phoneme—units which themselves consist of two or more phonemes—but smaller than the syllable. It is usually possible to divide a syllable into two parts, an opening and an end section. The word "string", for example, has a clear beginning in its first three consonants, "str", and an equally clear end section which contains the vowel and the last two consonants, "ing". This monosyllabic word, therefore, can be broken up into two phonological units, each made up of more than one phoneme. Units of this sort lie somewhere between a phoneme and a syllable, and are sometimes called "intra-syllabic units". The opening unit is often called "the onset" and the end unit "the rime".

There is a good reason for calling the end unit "the rime". Words rhyme when they share common rimes. "String" rhymes with "wing" and with "thing", and all three words have the same rime. This intrasyllabic unit therefore has an immense significance: rhyme is an extremely important part of our everyday lives. Rhymes are to be found practically everywhere—in poems, in songs, in advertisements and in political slogans. They are also a significant part of young children's lives. Long before children go to school, they are taught rhymes, and begin to make up their own (Chukovsky, 1963; Dowker, 1989; MacLean, Bryant & Bradley, 1987).

Just as the rime tends to consist of two or more phonemes, so the written version of this speech sound usually contains more than one letter. The sound which "cat" and "hat" share contains two phonemes: but these words share a common spelling sequence "-at" which represents the shared sound, and that sequence consists of two letters. So if children connect rhyming sounds with reading, the connection will be between particular sounds and sequences of letters.

At this point we ought to return to our central term "phonological awareness". Obviously someone who can explicitly report the sounds in any word is "aware" phonologically. But we have begun to extend the use of the term "awareness" by introducing the subject of rhyme. In our view, a child who recognises that two words rhyme and therefore have a sound in common must possess a degree of phonological awareness, even if it is not certain that this child can say exactly what is the sound that these words share. To know that there are categories of words ("cat", "hat" and "mat") which end with the same sound is a form of phonological awareness.

We now have two possible links between the constituent sounds in monosyllabic words and alphabetic letters. The first is the link between single letters and sounds which are usually phonemes, and the second is the link between the speech units, onset and rime, which often contain more than one phoneme and also are represented by a letter sequence like "-at" or "-ight" or "-ing". The difference between these two possible connections between phonological awareness and reading will play an important role in our book.

CAUSE AND EFFECT IN THE RELATIONSHIPS BETWEEN PHONOLOGICAL AWARENESS AND READING

We will show later that there is plenty of evidence for a connection between children's reading and their awareness of sounds. The better they are at reading, the more sensitive they seem to be to a word's constituent sounds. But connections of this sort always raise questions of cause and effect. There are at least two possibilities.

One is that children learn how to divide words up into their constituent sounds because they are taught to do so when they learn to read. In this case the experience of learning to read would be the cause of phonological awareness. The second possibility is that cause and effect go the other way round. Before children learn to read, they may build up phonological skills which then affect how well they learn to read.

Predictions

At first sight the two alternatives seem equally plausible. We can think of no pressing *a priori* reasons for preferring one hypothesis over the other. But at least one can find out which is right, for the two hypotheses produce radically different predictions.

1. Illiterate and Literate Groups.   One sharp difference between the two hypotheses is that they produce different predictions about people who have never learned to read. If reading is the main cause of phonological awareness, illiterates should be quite unable to succeed in tasks which test their awareness of sounds. Literate people, in contrast, should find these phonological tasks quite easy. On the other hand, if phonological awareness precedes reading then illiterate people should be as good in phonological tasks as anyone else.

2. Logographic and Alphabetic Groups.   Another way of distinguishing between the two hypotheses is to look at people who have not learned an alphabetic language—at those, for example, who have learned a script such as Chinese in which each word is represented by its own distinctive shape (a logogram), (see Fig. 1.2.) According to the first hypothesis (reading causes phonological awareness), there should be a considerable difference between these people who have learned a logographic script and thus have not been taught to divide words into sounds and others who have learned an alphabetic script: the "logographic" group should fare much worse than the "alphabetic group" in phonological tasks. But if the second hypothesis (phonological awareness affects reading) is right, there is no reason for this sort of difference between the two groups: the logographic group should have the same

| Chung | Pi | Hsiao | Pên | P'ing |
| (middle) | (to finish) | (small) | (root) | (level) |

FIG. 1.2.   Examples of Chinese characters.

phonological skills as those who have learned an alphabetic script. However, we have
to be a bit cautious here, because the comparison is not a pure one. Some of the
traditional Chinese characters contain "phonetics" which indicate part of their sound.

3. Younger and Older Children.   So far we have only talked about special
groups (if millions of Chinese readers can be called a special group). But, the two
hypotheses also lead to radically different predictions about the course of development
of phonological skills during childhood. Causes should precede effects, and so if
children become aware of sounds as a direct result of being taught to read they should
show no signs of phonological awareness until they have made some headway with
reading. But, according to the alternative hypothesis that children's phonological
awareness has an effect on the way that they learn to read, they should be able to
segment words into sounds before they learn to read.

1. DATA ON ILLITERATE PEOPLE

There would be little point in comparing illiterate with literate people in a country like
England, where instruction in reading is readily available, and illiteracy comparatively
unusual. In such a country illiterate people may well have other problems than just a
failure to read, and so any difference between a literate and an illiterate group may
have nothing to do with reading as such, and may simply reflect social and economic
differences. However, there are many countries where illiteracy is more common, and
the teaching of reading less widespread. In these countries it is easier to find groups
of literate and illiterate people who are like each other in every way except that the
people in one group can read and those in the other cannot.

One such country used to be Portugal in the 1970s before the time of a radical and
effective programme to remove the problem of illiteracy. At that time Morais, Cary,
Alegria and Bertelson (1979) studied a group of Portuguese illiterates and compared
them to a similar group of adults who had been illiterate but had learned to read in

adult literacy programmes. The experimenters gave both groups two tasks. One was to add a sound to a word ("alhaco"–"palhaco"), and the other to subtract a sound from a word ("purso"–"urso"). These examples are real meaningful words, but some of the addition and deletion problems involved made-up nonsense words.

Although the people in the illiterate group were able to manage some of the words (46% success in the addition task with real words), they made many more mistakes in the phonological tasks than the literate people did. The illiterate people did particularly badly when nonsense words were involved. One can note straightaway that at the very least this remarkable study demonstrates that one cannot take phonological awareness for granted. Here was a group of effective and competent adults who were strikingly insensitive to distinctions which most of us find transparently obvious.

Morais and his colleagues concluded that this was good evidence for the first of the two possible hypotheses, that people become aware of the sounds in words as a result of learning to read. However, we should like to suggest some reasons for caution about the authors' main conclusion. The first is that one cannot be sure that the two groups were equivalent in every way apart from the fact that those in one could read and those in the other could not. It seems unlikely that pure chance alone determined whether or not these people took adult literacy courses. There could certainly have been some self-selection, and that could have been influenced by the people's different abilities.

The second worry is that the biggest difference between the two groups was in the nonsense word condition. This raises the possibility that their problem was not so much with the business of adding and deleting phonemes, but with nonsense words *per se*. We need to give these people other tasks which involve nonsense words but no phonological analysis. According to the Morais et al. (1979) hypothesis the illiterates would have no particular difficulty in such tasks.

The third and most troublesome problem with the study is that all the tasks in it involved judgements about phonemes: for that reason the experiment is not a good test of the hypothesis about awareness of phonemes. The fact that the illiterate people were worse in all four tasks may mean, as the authors claim, that they have a specific insensitivity to phonemes, but it could also mean that they are worse at manipulating anything or at understanding instructions or at paying attention or even at caring how well they did. Single condition experiments are not the right way to test specific hypotheses.

Fortunately, the Brussels group has gone a long way towards checking that the effects are specific ones in another experiment in which they did include conditions which did not involve phonemes (Morais, Cluytens, Alegria & Content, 1986a). Once again they compared a group of illiterate Portuguese people to others who also had been illiterate but who by that time had with varying degrees of success completed a literacy course. The people in both groups were given a set of tasks, some of which involved phonemes and others not. The experimenters' prediction was that the illiterate group would be at a large disadvantage in the phoneme tasks, but no worse than the literate group in the other conditions.

The experiment was a complicated one, because all the people being studied in it were given several tasks. The most interesting comparisons were between tasks in which the unit was the phoneme and others in which it was the syllable. One of these comparisons was between two "deletion" tasks; all the people were given both a phoneme and a syllable deletion task. These were somewhat limited tasks since they involved only nonsense words and the unit to be detached—phoneme or syllable—was always the same one. In the phoneme task the subjects were given a series of nonsense words beginning with "p" and had to work out what they would sound like without that opening consonant. In the syllable task the opening sound that had to be removed was the vowel "u" (this vowel was always followed by a consonant, and so its removal did shorten the word by a whole syllable).

The illiterate people were worse than the others at both tasks, but they were at a much greater disadvantage in the phoneme task than they were in the syllable task. This, the authors concluded, showed that illiterate people are relatively insensitive to phonemes. But one needs to be cautious about this conclusion too.

For one thing it is a pity that Morais and his colleagues used only nonsense words because these seem to give a particularly low estimate of illiterate people's sensitivity to phonemes. For another, the phoneme that had to be deleted was always a consonant and yet the syllable that had to be deleted was always a vowel. Because of this the difference between the two tasks may have been nothing to do with phonemes and syllables; the illiterates might simply have found it easier to cope with vowels than with consonants. Finally, there is the awkward fact that the illiterate group were worse also in the syllable task. Does this mean that the effects of literacy are not as specific as the Brussels group originally claimed?

We have some of the same worries about the other syllable/phoneme comparison. Here the task was to listen to a series of sentences and to say when a particular sound (sometimes a phoneme, sometimes a syllable) occurred. Once again the illiterates were much worse than the others when it came to phonemes, but they also made more mistakes than the literate people in the syllable task. There were vast differences between the two groups in both kinds of task.

There were other tasks which did not involve judgements about phonemes. One involved rhyme: The task was to say which two out of a set of five words rhymed. Rhyming tasks, as we have already noted, are phonological in that to understand that "cat" and "mat" rhyme, you must be able to divide each monosyllabic word into segments. However, these segments are usually larger units than single phonemes; the common segment "-at" in this example contains two phonemes. So if the detection of single phonemes is the stumbling block for non-literate people, rhymes should not be too difficult for them.

But here too the illiterate people were at a noticeable disadvantage. Their scores were more than 20% worse than those of the people in the other group. So the difficulties of the illiterate group are not confined to phonemes; these people are worse at detecting "rimes" as well.

In fact, the only segmentation task in which the illiterate group did not fall far behind the others was the music task. This was a deletion task which involved no speech but was in other ways equivalent to the other two deletion tests. The experimenters played a four-note tune to the subjects, who then had to sing back the last three notes. Here at any rate the illiterate people were no worse than the rest. But the trouble with this result is that the task was an extremely difficult one for both groups. It is just possible that one group might have been better than the other at segmenting sequences of music, but that the task was so hard that people could not show how good they were at this kind of segmentation.

The research by Morais and his colleagues that we have described so far shows that illiterate people have a great deal of difficulty with phonological tasks, but it does not pin their difficulties down to phonemes. Whatever the form of their phonological difficulties, we still have to wonder whether the only way round them is to learn how to read. That was the original idea of Morais and his colleagues, but in another study (Morais, Content, Bertelson, Cary & Kolinsky, 1988) they managed to show that there are other ways to help illiterate people to do better in a phonological task. In this experiment they worked only with illiterate Portuguese adults. The experimenters gave these people a deletion task, in which they were asked to delete either a consonant (fak-ak) or a vowel (aki-ki) from a nonsense word. But this time Morais et al. (1988) told the people being tested whether their responses were correct or not.

The scores in this study were high—89% correct on the syllable task and 69% correct on the final set of trials in the phoneme task. Half of these illiterate people were right in three-quarters of the phoneme deletion trials in the last block of eight trials, although two of the people in the group never learned to cope with the phoneme deletion task. This rapid improvement by most of the illiterate people in the study after a little instruction and feedback is quite striking. It made Morais and his colleagues wonder "whether the degree of segmental analysis ability that is reached with the present sort of training procedures is relevant to reading acquisition" (p. 351). The result means that there is more than one way to help an illiterate person to be aware of sounds. The experience of learning to read may make people aware of sounds, but there are other ways as well to promote this awareness.

2. STUDIES OF PEOPLE WHO READ NON-ALPHABETIC SCRIPTS

The ideas of the Brussels group have received strong support from work on a very different set of people. Read, Zhang, Nie and Ding (1986) took advantage of the fact that some Chinese people have been taught an alphabetic version of written Chinese (pinyin) as well as the traditional Chinese orthography which is logographic. The authors compared a group of people taught pinyin with another group who had learned only the traditional scripts in tasks which were the exact equivalents of the original Morais et al. (1979) tests.

The results of the study were strikingly similar to those of the original experiment by Morais and his colleagues. One simply has to substitute "pinyin" for "literate" and "non-pinyin" for "illiterate". The people in the "pinyin" group did far better than those who had only learned the traditional logographic script in both tasks. And this difference between the groups was more pronounced with nonsense words than with real words.

Here is the authors' main conclusion about these results: "It is not literacy in general which leads to segmentation skill, but alphabetic literacy in particular" (p. 41). But, because this study took an identical form to the original Morais et al. (1986a) experiment, we need to be cautious again. Read and his colleagues left the same gap in their study as Morais et al. had done. Their tasks were just phoneme tasks. We need to know how well the "non-pinyin" group would handle syllable and rhyme tasks before we can accept the authors' conclusion that these people have a specific difficulty with phonemes.

It is also possible that the two groups were not really comparable. Pinyin was introduced into Chinese schools in the late 1940s. This means that on the whole the "non-pinyin" people had been to school before this time and so were relatively old. The discrepancy in the two groups' ages was quite considerable (mean ages of 49 years and 33 years). The "non-pinyin" people also had had three years less schooling than the people in the other group (ten years vs. seven years). Both these factors, age and amount of education, could have made a difference.

We have another comparison between an "alphabetic" and a "non-alphabetic" group to describe. Virginia Mann (1986) compared American with Japanese schoolchildren. She did this because Japanese children do not learn an alphabet when they start to learn to read. Japanese writing consists of two types of script, kanji, which are the old Chinese logograms, and kana, in which each letter/symbol represents a syllable. Syllabaries are interesting because they are phonological in nature but do not deal in phonemes. So anyone who holds the hypothesis that reading leads to awareness of phonemes should predict that Japanese children would be less sensitive than their Western counterparts to phonemes.

Mann's interesting study shows this to be true of younger children. She gave the Japanese six year olds two kinds of task. In one the experimenter said a word to the child and the child had to tap out the number of sounds in the word with a hammer. There were two versions of this tapping task. In one the children had to tap out the "mora" which are roughly equivalent to syllables. So the children had to tap twice to the word "hito", three times to "hitotsu" and four times to "hitotsubu". The other version was a phoneme tapping task: the child had to tap out the number of phonemes in each word, which meant two taps to "ho", three to "hon", and so on. Mann's other test was a deletion task which was rather like the ones that we have described already. The children had to work out what a word would sound like without its initial mora (syllable) or without its initial phoneme.

These six year old children found both phoneme tasks extremely difficult and were much worse at them than at the mora (syllable) tasks. When Mann compared their scores to comparable scores produced by American six year olds she found that the American children did much better than the Japanese in the phoneme tasks, and that there was not much difference between the two when it came to tapping or deleting syllables. Here again is strong support for the idea that children become aware of phonemes as a result of being taught an alphabet.

However, Mann also gave versions of the phoneme tapping and deletion tasks to some older Japanese children and found that they were rather successful. Children around the ages of nine and ten years who, according to Mann, had never been taught an alphabet nevertheless coped with the task quite well. Their success, together with the relative failure of the younger Japanese children, gives us two very clear messages. One is that the experience of learning an alphabetic script does promote awareness of phonemes. The other is that there are other ways as well to become aware of phonemes. These, of course, are the two conclusions that we drew from the work on illiterate people.

But we are left with an awkward problem. If Japanese ten year olds do so well in phoneme tasks, why did these tasks defeat the Chinese adults in Read et al.'s (1986) "non-pinyin" group? How are we to explain this discrepancy? One possibility is that the Japanese children did have the benefit of a genuinely phonological script, albeit one which deals in syllables. In fact, Japanese children apparently are taught the kana (syllabic) symbols in a way that might well encourage them to think about phonemes as well as about syllables. It seems that Japanese teachers often draw their pupils' attention to the fact that different kana start in the same way (ka, ko, ki) as others and end in the same way (ka, na, ta) as others. Thus the teacher actually shows the children how to group these syllabic symbols on the basis of shared phonemes. This kind of experience might be the reason why Japanese 10 year olds seem to be more sensitive to phonemes than many Chinese literate adults.

3. THE DEVELOPMENT OF PHONOLOGICAL AWARENESS IN CHILDHOOD

The timing of phonological awareness and of reading must be an important part of this debate. If the experience of learning to read produces phonological awareness, then children will only become aware of the constituent sounds in words after they have begun to learn to read. But one would expect them to detect and recognise these constituent sounds quite some time before they can read, if cause and effect go the other way round and children's awareness of sounds is a major influence on their success in reading.

The answer to this apparently simple "before or after" question is actually quite complicated and also very interesting. A lot turns on the form of phonological awareness being studied, for it turns out that children do well in some phonological tests long before they learn to read, and yet fail others dismally until the time that they go to school. For this reason we will look at their performance in different phonological tasks separately.

The Deletion and Elision task. What would "stand" sound like without the "t"?

One of the main reasons for thinking that children become aware of the sounds in words as a direct result of learning to read is that they do extremely badly in some phonological tasks before they can read and continue to find these tasks difficult for some time after they have begun to read, even though the tasks seem transparently easy to literate adults. The most striking example is the phoneme deletion or elision task (Fig. 1.3) which was originally devised by Bruce (1964). It was through Bruce's research that we first learned not to take phonological awareness for granted in young children.

Bruce worked with children whose mental ages ranged from five to nine years. He gave them three different tasks, in each of which they had to work out what particular words would sound like if they lost a specific phoneme. In every trial the experimenter said a word, and then told the child the sound that had to be deleted from it. In one task the children had to "remove" the first sound (e.g. JAM-AM) of a set of words, in another a middle sound (e.g. SNAIL-SAIL), and in a third the last sound (e.g. FORK-FOR).

These apparently simple tasks were not at all simple for the younger children in the study. The mean scores out of a possible 30 for the five and six year old groups were only 0 (*none* of the 5 year olds produced the right answer in *any* of the 30 trials) and 1.8, respectively. Even the seven year olds only managed 8.75 correct answers in the 30 trials. Only children with a mental age of eight or nine years managed a reasonable performance (16.4 and 26.7 respectively). In this way Bruce demonstrated that young children stumble surprisingly badly when they have to make phonological judgements that depend on an explicit awareness of phonemes.

It is difficult to overestimate the importance of Bruce's results. There is no doubt about them; they have been confirmed many times since he originally published his study. Yet they still retain something of their original surprise. That surprise lies in the

Deletion: end sound	Deletion: first sound	Elision: middle sound
1. *Syllable*	1. *Onset*	1. *Part of onset*
party-part	near-ear	snail-sail
fairy-fair	cold-old	frog-fog
every-ever	nice-ice	
	hill-ill	
2. *Part of rime*	2. *Part of onset*	2. *Rime*
think-thin	spin-pin	hand-had
farm-far	frock-rock	nest-net
tent-ten	stop-top	lost-lot
start-star	plate-late	went-wet
pink-pin		left-let

FIG. 1.3.   Deletion and elision tasks (Bruce, 1964).

clear demonstration of a radical difference between young schoolchildren and the adults who bring them up and, among other things, have to teach them to read.

Deleting the Onset: "pies" to "eyes"

When someone shows a surprising intellectual weakness in young children, as Bruce did, others naturally look for special circumstances in which children overcome this weakness. The onset-rime distinction suggests one possible circumstance. It is possible that the children found Bruce's task difficult because in most trials they had to manipulate segments which were only part of the onset (SNAIL-SAIL) or only part of the rime (FORK-FOR). The task might have been a great deal easier if it had consisted only of trials in which one of these two speech units had to be detached and the other left intact.

As it happens, an experiment of this sort was carried out by Calfee (1977), though he did not describe it in terms of onset and rime. He asked a large number of five and six year old children to play a game, resembling Pig Latin, in which the children had to "strip" the initial phoneme from each word. Calfee told them: "When I say 'greet', you should say 'eat'; when I say 'ties', you should say 'eyes' ", and so on. Notice that the children had to "strip" the onset and leave the rime.

After some training trials ("If I say 'pies', you point and say 'eyes' "), the children were given transfer tests. In one test the children were given new words to segment, but the correct answers were the same as before (e.g. "spies-eyes"). Later tests involved new answers (e.g. "mice-ice").

The children did extremely well during the training. They were right in over 90% of trials. Their scores in the transfer tests were also very high: on average they got the right answer well over 80% of the time in these tests. The children's age made no difference: the five year olds did as well as the six year olds. So here is clear evidence that children can delete a single phoneme in a word provided that this phoneme is the onset of the word.

The results of an experiment by Content, Morais, Alegria and Bertelson (1982) can be explained in much the same way. They asked some five year old children, who were not yet at school, to delete the initial phoneme in a series of words. The task that they gave these children took the form of a game in which puppets spoke an invented language. One puppet kept making a mistake which the other puppet corrected. The mistake was to put an extra phoneme at the beginning of the word, and that had to be removed. After a while the children were asked to take over from the second puppet and correct the mistake themselves. So they had to delete the initial phoneme in every word spoken by the first puppet.

The words whose first sound had to be deleted were of three types: some began with a vowel, others with a fricative consonant and others with a plosive consonant. The vowel that had to be removed always represented a whole syllable. But the consonants that had to be deleted were the words' onsets. The words were French, but the English equivalent of the vowel task would be "apart-part", and of the consonant task, "beak-eak".

The children were very good at deleting initial vowels. In fact they did this correctly 81% of the time. But they were less successful at deleting initial fricatives (20% correct) or plosives (42% correct). However, they were then given some training on phonemic manipulation and blending, and as a result their performance in the two consonant tasks improved dramatically—by roughly 40% in each case. A group of children who received no training did not improve in this way. In some follow-up tests given six months later the children who were trained still did better in these tasks than those who were not.

So this study, like Calfee's, shows us that children who have made little or no progress in learning to read nevertheless cope well when they have to delete a phoneme from a word, provided that this phoneme represents the onset of the word and provided too that some care is taken to orient them to the task. The experiment also demonstrates that children have relatively little difficulty when they have to detect and remove a syllable (the vowel condition).

Deleting the Last Sound—A Special Case?

There is another exception to Bruce's dictum that young children find it nearly impossible to work out what a word sounds like if a single phoneme is detached from it, but this exception may have very little to do with explicit phonological awareness. Children do quite well if you ask them to say a word, but to stop before they have said it all. This was first noted by Fox and Routh (1975) who asked children, aged from three to seven years, to "say just a little bit" of either a sentence, a word, or a single syllable. Thus there were three tasks: saying the first word in a sentence ("Peter" out of "Peter jumps"); saying the first syllable in a word ("Pete" in "Peter"); and saying the first phoneme in a syllable ("Pe" in "Pete").

The children managed the sentence and word tasks very well. Even the three year olds were right in around 60% of the trials in these two tasks. From four years on the children made hardly any mistakes. The phoneme task, in contrast, was much harder, but the three year old children managed to be right 25% of the time. The four year olds were correct 60% of the time, and by the age of five to seven years performance was 85–95% correct.

There are two things to be said about these results. The first is that, despite some clear differences with Bruce's study, the results actually provide further support for Bruce's position. Fox and Routh's study demonstrates that the children find it particularly difficult to "remove" phonemes: other speech units, words and syllables, do not cause them any particular problem. The difficulty is a specific one.

The second point is that the apparent divergence from Bruce's results—the quite reasonable level of performance in the difficult phoneme task—actually extends our knowledge about children's phonological skills in an interesting way. There are two possible reasons for the children's relative success in this task. One is that the phoneme that they had to produce usually coincided with the word's onset. The other is that stopping short of saying a whole word—arresting the word in mid-stream, so to speak—may be a particularly easy task for young children and one that requires no phonological awareness at all. The child may simply need to know that he must start saying the word in a certain way, but then stop at a certain point before finishing it.

This may be the reason for the results of another, rather similar, study in which children showed that they were able to say most of the word and to omit its ending, even when this meant that they had to segment the word's rime. Rosner and Simon (1971) gave children, whose ages ranged from five years (kindergarten) to eleven years, different deletion tasks, including some in which they had to omit the final consonant of a one-syllable word (e.g. "belt" → "bel"), or to omit the initial consonant of a one-syllable word (e.g. "lend" → "end"). The children in the youngest groups (five and six year olds) did a great deal better when they had to say all of the word except for its last sound than when they had to omit the first sound. Still another experiment has produced much the same result. Content, Kolinsky, Morais and Bertelson (1986) asked four and five year old "preliterate" children to work out what words would sound like if their opening consonant or their end consonant were removed. They gave these children the same puppet game as Content et al. (1982) had done before. Once again the children did quite well in both tasks, but managed the end sound problem with fewer mistakes.

The results of the Rosner and Simon study and of the Content et al. experiment seem at first not to fit at all well with the onset-rime distinction, because in both cases the children did better in a task in which they had to manipulate only part of the rime. However, it is possible that "manipulate" is the wrong word here. We cannot be sure that the children knew what the end sound actually was when they omitted it. They could, as we mentioned in our discussion of the Fox and Routh (1975) study, simply have learned that they had to produce an incomplete word which meant stopping just before the end.

Conclusions about Deletion

The experiments which began with Bruce's pioneering study have revealed two facts of great interest. One is that young children, particularly children who have not yet learned to read, are in great difficulty in tasks in which they have to detect and manipulate phonemes. Their frequent mistakes in these tasks fit well with the results of the studies that we have already reviewed on adults who have not learned an alphabetic script and who also find it extremely difficult to isolate and detect single phonemes.

The second contribution of the deletion studies has been to demonstrate that some phonemes nevertheless are reasonably easy for young children to detect. Children manage quite well when they have to delete the onset of a word and leave the rime intact, even when the onset is just a single phoneme, as long as they are given some training to do so (Calfee, 1977).

ONE-TO-ONE CORRESPONDENCE TASKS

Bruce's opinion that young schoolchildren are at first quite unable to analyse words into their component sounds was shared by the well known group from the Haskins laboratory. It was they who devised the much used phonological tapping test (Fig. 1.4) (Liberman et al., 1974), which we have already mentioned when we described the Mann study. In this, children have to learn to tap out the sounds in words spoken to them by the experimenter. Usually the children are given two tasks. In one they have to tap out the number of syllables in each word that is spoken to them. So "elephant" would need three taps and "money" two. The other task is a phoneme task: the children have to tap out the number of phonemes in each word—three taps for "cat" and two for "in".

The Haskins group found that it is easier for young children to tap out the syllables than the phonemes. Most five year old children found the phoneme task impossible. If this task is a test of the awareness of phonemes then young children do not have this awareness.

That indeed was the Haskins group's conclusion, but before we accept it we ought to look at the other demands—over and above the analysis of phonemes—made by their phoneme task. The most obvious is this. The child has to go through a form of counting or one-to-one correspondence (three taps for three phonemes, two taps for two) in each trial; and yet there is plenty of evidence to show that one-to-one correspondence is not perfectly understood by children of five or even six years (Piaget, 1952; Fuson, 1988). Could this have been the reason for the younger children's abysmal performance?

At first sight this alternative seems quite implausible, because of the same children's comparative success with the syllable task. That task also seems to involve one-to-one

Syllables		
One tap	*Two taps*	*Three taps*
box	dinner	popsicle
cook	open	valentine
green	birthday	president
jump	chicken	gasoline
dog	letter	cucumber
Phoneme		
i	my	red
e	so	soap
u	he	pot
o	up	heat
/ae/	at	book

FIG. 1.4.   The tapping task (Liberman et al., 1974).

correspondence and yet even five year old children managed it reasonably well. However, there is a possible reason for their success in the syllable task which would leave the objection about the cognitive demands of the phoneme task intact. Tapping is a rhythmic activity and the rhythm of a word is captured in its syllables. When a child produces three taps for "elephant" she may simply be saying the word to herself again and be reproducing its rhythm as she does so. In the phoneme task, on the other hand, she may have to work out the number of phonemes first and only then tap that number out. So the two tasks might impose quite different extra cognitive demands.

There is one further experiment which seems to take care of this objection. Treiman and Baron (1981) gave children both the phoneme and the syllable tests, but in a new form: instead of tapping, the children had to lay out tokens—one for each syllable in the syllable task and one for each phoneme in the phoneme task. Laying out tokens does not seem like a rhythmic task, and yet the results of this experiment were the same as those in the Haskins group's study. Once again the syllable task was the easier of the two, and once again the five year olds had some success with this syllable task—but they had no success at all with the phoneme test. This is good evidence that the relative difficulty of the phoneme task is, as the Haskins group originally suggested, due to young children's insensitivity to single phonemes.

The Phoneme Tapping Task and
Knowledge of Spelling

The fact that children who cannot yet read have such difficulty with one-to-one correspondence tapping tasks fits in well with the idea that children become aware of phonemes after they learn to read and probably as a result of the experience of reading. Two other studies with this kind of task provide stronger and more direct support for this idea.

One is an experiment by Ehri and Wilce (1980). Words which have the same number of phonemes are not always spelled the same way. Some have more letters than others. "Pitch" has one more letter than "rich", even though both contain the same number of phonemes. If children eventually manage one-to-one correspondence tasks as a direct result of their experience of learning to read and spell, their judgements might reflect the number of letters rather than the number of phonemes in the word. Ehri and Wilce set out to find if this was so by giving nine and ten year old children pairs of words which sounded similar but were spelled differently, such as "pitch", "rich", "new", and "do". The children had to represent each phoneme by a counter. They were also asked to spell these words afterwards. Ehri and Wilce found the effect that they were looking for. The children tended to assign more counters to the words with larger numbers of letters. The children were more likely to make this mistake if they knew how to spell the words properly.

This result was confirmed by Tunmer and Nesdale (1985). They asked six year old children to tap out the number of sounds in real words and nonsense words. Some of the words contained digraphs which represented a single phoneme (e.g. "book"); others (e.g. "man") did not. Tunmer and Nesdale predicted that children would make "overshoot errors" (i.e. extra taps) with the words which contained digraphs. This is what happened. So both studies show that children use what knowledge they have of spelling sequences when they are given phoneme tasks of this sort. They tap out letters. Their route to phonemes is through the letters which represent them.

HOW LONG IS "CROCODILE"?

The more phonemes there are in a word, the longer, on the whole, that word is. If children are aware of the constituent sounds in words they ought to have some idea about the relative length of different words. They should recognise that the word "bicycle" is longer than the word "car", even though the object "car" is generally a great deal longer than the object "bicycle". As a measure of children's phonological awareness comparisons of the length of spoken words are a great deal cruder than the Haskins tapping test (one cannot tell whether the children are judging phonemes or syllables, for example), but the tasks seem to be getting at the same kind of phonological knowledge.

The first attempt to see how well children judge the relative length of different words was made by Sinclair and Papandropoulou, who were colleagues of Jean Piaget. In one of his later books, *The Grasp of Consciousness* (1978), Piaget had argued that children often succeed in some task or solve some problem without being explicitly aware of how they do so. The instances that he dealt with in his book involved motor skills, for the most part. However, Sinclair and Papandropoulou saw that his ideas about awareness could be applied to phonology as well. Young children, they argued, can distinguish different words on the basis of phonemes without being aware of these phonemes in much the same way as they can crawl if they want to but could not possibly tell you about the sequence of hand and knee positions involved in crawling.

Papandropoulou asked children to think of and say a long or a short word (Berthoud-Papandropoulou, 1978), and she reported that at five and even sometimes at six years of age they seemed to confuse the physical meaning of the word with its sound. "Armoire" (cupboard) is a long word "because it has a lot of things in it". "Primevere" (primrose), in contrast, is given as a short word, no doubt because primroses are small flowers. When they are a little older, at around six and seven years, and have had some experience with reading, children's answers are less erratic but appear to be about the number of letters in words rather than about their physical auditory length. Sometimes this concern with letters has amusing results. One child gave a "typewriter" as an example of a long word "because it has lots of letters", and another offered "a newspaper" with the comment that newspapers contain "a lot of written stuff".

These two results—first that young children are bad at distinguishing long from short words, and second that when they do judge length on the basis of something other than the word's meaning they turn to its orthography—again suggest an awareness which follows and is influenced by the experience of learning to read. But there are grounds for caution about this conclusion. The trouble is that it is not at all clear that the children really understood the question which Papandropoulou put to them. The results of her experiment do not rule out another possibility, which is that they are explicitly aware of these sounds but do not connect them to "length". In the child's experience the words "long" and "short" will have been used in connection with distance and with time, but almost certainly not with the duration of single words. There was no check in the experiment that a child who was aware of sounds necessarily understood that this was what the question was about, and in fact it is difficult to see what that check could have been.

However, a similar study by Rozin, Bressman and Taft (1974) supports the idea that children do not readily connect the length of spoken words with the number of letters in words. They showed children two cards, each with a word or a nonsense sound on it. One of the words was a long one, and the other short. The experimenter said the two words and then asked the child which card contained which word. For example, the experimenter said "One of these words says 'mow'. Say 'mow'. The other says 'motorcycle'. Say 'motorcycle'. Now point to the word which says 'motorcycle' ". On half of the trials the long word was the target, on the other half the short word.

Kindergartners (six year olds) varied in their ability to perform the task, but some were very poor indeed: Only 8–11% of "urban kindergartners" were successful compared to 43% of "suburban kindergartners": the rest of the children were at chance level. So children take time to learn that a long word will have a large number of letters in it. But this of course does not necessarily mean that they take equally long to realise that long words generally contain more phonemes than shorter ones do. Papandropoulou's idea still needs a proper test.

ONSET AND RIME AND LEVELS OF PHONOLOGICAL AWARENESS

When people talk about phonological awareness, they usually acknowledge that there may be different levels of this awareness. As we have seen, many of the studies of this question make an explicit distinction between the awareness of syllables and the awareness of phonemes. The distinction plays an important part in the claims made by those who think that reading determines phonological awareness. In fact, their argument is usually just about phonemes, and they are quite prepared to admit that children can manipulate syllables consciously before they learn to read.

On the whole, the results that we have discussed so far support this distinction and the general idea that explicit knowledge about syllables precedes reading while an awareness of phonemes follows it. Put like this, the evidence does seem to support the notion that reading causes phonological awareness rather than the other way around. It is easy to argue that knowledge of sounds which is restricted to whole syllables is not likely to be much use when it comes to learning an alphabetic script, where the critical segments are small units. This is a plausible argument, but is not necessarily correct. Children's awareness of syllables might affect their progress in learning to read; the syllable too is an important unit in reading. The question can only be settled empirically.

But there is a danger to the emphasis on children's awareness of only two phonological units, the phoneme and the syllable. What about onset and rime? Are young children aware of onsets and rimes and do they find it easier to detect these "intrasyllabic units" than phonemes? The question is important because it has serious implications about the kind of connection that children make between sounds and letters. If it is just a matter of phonemes, then the connections between sounds and writing will be connections between single sounds and single letters —grapheme-phoneme connections. But if children are aware of onsets and rimes and connect these intra-syllabic speech units to writing, they must be making connections between sounds and whole sequences of letters. In written words onsets and rimes—particularly rimes—are often represented by strings of letters, like "str" and "ing".

The psychologist who did most to draw our attention to the significance of the hitherto neglected intra-syllabic units was Rebecca Treiman. She demonstrated that people find it easier to segment syllables into onset and rime than into units which cut across onset and rime. Her original work on this topic was with adults (Treiman, 1983), but then she turned her attention to children (Treiman, 1985a).

In one experiment she played a game with a group of eight year old children: she said a word and they had to substitute part of that word with another sound. Sometimes the child had to delete the opening two phonemes of the word spoken by the experimenter; in some cases ("lug" for "fog") this involved breaking up the rime and in others ("slu" for "fru") preserving it. At other times it was the last two phonemes that had to be changed, and sometimes ("fli" for "fru") this involved breaking up the onset and at others ("ful" for "fog") preserving it. Treiman found that the children managed much better when the onset or rime was preserved than when it was not. This is good evidence that for eight year old children at any rate the division between onset and rime is an easy one, and thus that it is reasonable to claim that they are aware of sounds at an intra-syllabic level.

Eight years, however, is quite old as far as this discussion is concerned. We really need to know whether the onset-rime distinction is also an important one for children who are just beginning to read. Do five year olds who are plainly aware of syllables but are usually in some difficulties when they have to respond to phonemes perceive and use the division between the onset and rime of a single syllable? Are they also aware of sounds at an intra-syllabic level? Treiman claimed that they are.

She devised another game for children aged between four and a half and six years. She showed them a puppet which, she said, had a favourite sound. The children had to judge whether some nonsense words contained this sound. Part of the time the sound was "s", at other times "f". The sound was always at the beginning of the words in which it occurred ("sa", "san", "sna"), and was either the complete onset ("sa", "san"), or part of the onset ("sna"). Treiman predicted that it would be easier for the children to identify the sound when it formed the complete onset than when it did not. Her prediction turned out to be right: it was twice as difficult for them to disentangle the "s" sound in words like "sna" than in the "sa" or "san" words.

Treiman's idea about why the children found the "sna" task difficult is certainly plausible, but her explanation is not watertight. The problem here is that double consonants may be particularly hard to disentangle. That on its own would explain Treiman's results, and it is an entirely different explanation from hers. One needs additional tasks in which children had to recognise consonants which are only part of the rime ("s" in "wes" or in "wesp"); in both examples the child would have to break up the rime to isolate the "s" sound.

Fortunately, there is another quite simple way to find out whether the onset-rime division plays an important part in children's reading. It is to look at the way in which children judge whether different words begin or end with the same sound as each other. One way to do this is to give children an oddity task—a task in which they have to say which one out of three words is the odd one because it does not contain a sound which is shared by the other two words.

Suppose that the words are "doll", "deaf", and "can". Two of the words start with the same phoneme, and the third, "can", does not. If children can isolate onsets they should be able to work out which of the two words share the same phoneme and which is the odd one that does not, because two begin with the same onset and the odd word begins in another way.

In that example the important sound—shared by two words but not by the third—was the opening consonant. What about the closing consonant? If the words are "mop", "lead", and "whip", the crucial phoneme—the one shared by two of the words but not by the other—is only part of each word's rime. In fact, all three words have different rimes, as well as different onsets, from each other. The child has to break up the rime in each word in order to see that "mop" and "whip" end in the same sound. So this end sound task should be much the harder of the two, if children do indeed work out the words' onsets and rimes but cannot divide these units up any further.

Kirtley, Bryant, MacLean and Bradley (1989) gave a large group of five year old children both these oddity tasks, and found that the opening sound task ("doll", "deaf", "can") was indeed much easier than the end sound task ("mop", "lead", "whip") (Fig. 1.5). So these children seemed to be able to categorise words quite easily when they could use the words' onsets to do so, but not when they needed to break up the words' rimes. The onset-rime division seems to play a part in their awareness of sounds.

About half of these children could read no words at all at the time: the rest had made some headway in learning to read. Both groups did much better with the opening sound task than with the end sound task. But there was a difference between the readers and non-readers. The scores of the non-readers were at "chance level" in the end sound task—no better than if they had chosen quite randomly. On the other hand, the scores of the readers were still low on this task, but they were better than chance. They could disentangle the last sound to some extent. Yet they had only just begun to read. It looks as though the experience of learning to read may have had the fairly immediate effect of helping them to take apart the words' rime.

However, there is one other possible reason for the difficulty of the end sound task—an alternative to our idea that it is difficult because it involves breaking into the

Experiment 1

End sounds				First sounds			
1st	2nd	3rd	4th	1st	2nd	3rd	4th
1. pin	gun	*hat*	men	man	mint	*peck*	mug
2. red	*cup*	toad	bad	peg	*land*	pin	pot
3. *pen*	cut	sat	hot	*farm*	sand	sit	sun
4. peg	mug	dog	*can*	cow	can	cat	*pig*
5. lip	tap	*beg*	map	leaf	land	*spoon*	let
6. *met*	ball	sell	doll	*leg*	bus	band	boat
7. sit	dot	pet	*car*	top	tin	tag	*bed*

Experiment 2

Categorisation	Odd word	Opening sound	End sound
1. single C	different C	doll, deaf, *can*	mop, *lead*, whip
2. CV or VC	different C and V	*cap*, doll, dog	top, *rail*, hop

FIG. 1.5.   Design of the Kirtley et al. (1989) study.

rime. This other possibility is that all end sound tasks are difficult—that it is always harder to categorise words by the end sounds than by their beginning sounds. There is an easy way to test this alternative: it is to ask children to categorise words by their rimes. Give them a rime—or rhyme—oddity task. According to our ideas, it should be much easier to work out the odd word in "top", "rail", and "hop" than in "mop", "whip", and "lead". In the first case the two words which end in the same way rhyme, and therefore share the same rime: in the second case, as we have already seen, all three words have different rimes. The difference between the two tasks is simply that in the first case the two words which end in the same way have the vowel as well as the end consonant in common.

There is an interesting corollary to this argument. In the experiment that we have just described the words in the easy beginning sound task ("doll", "deaf", "can") all had different vowel sounds, and yet the children managed it very well. This, we think, is because the vowel sound has nothing to do with the onset. It follows that the children would find an opening sound task no easier when the words which begin in the same way share the same vowel as well ("cap", "doll", "dog") than when they all have different vowels ("doll", "deaf", "can").

Both these predictions were tested in an experiment (also reported in the Kirtley et al., 1989 study) with five, six and seven year old children, and both were fulfilled. The addition of a common vowel ("top", "rail", "hop") made the end sound task much easier: It made much less difference to the opening sound task ("cap", "doll", "dog").

It seems to us that the only possible explanation for these results is the idea with which we started. Young children who are at the beginning stages of reading can break up syllables into onsets and rimes with ease. This is the form of phonological awareness that comes naturally to them. They find it extremely difficult to detect phonemes, except when the phoneme coincides with the word's onset. Only then is phoneme detection easy for them.

RHYME AND ALLITERATION

Our discussion of onset and rime naturally leads us to the question of children's awareness of rhyme and alliteration. Words which have the same rimes, as we have already remarked, are rhyming words, just as words which share an onset are alliterative. So if children are aware of onset and rime they should also be sensitive to rhyme and alliteration in the words that they hear.

To recognise that words rhyme is to put them into categories. These are categories of words, like "cat", "hat" and "mat", which share a common sound. If children do form such categories, these may well play an important part when they begin to read. Many words that rhyme are spelled in the same way too. This is true of "cat", "hat" and "mat" and of words with more complex spelling patterns like "light", "fight" and "tight".

It is quite possible that children use these categories when they learn about spelling patterns. They may learn that there are groups of words which rhyme and have the same spelling sequences, and presumably it is more economical to learn about groups of words with the same spelling pattern than to have to learn how each individual word is spelled. As well as this the existence of categories of words which rhyme and share a spelling sequence may make it possible for children to make inferences about new words. When they learn to read and spell the word "fight" they may to be able to use this knowledge to help them to read or to spell "light" because they know the words share a common sound. (This same knowledge might also get in their way when they try to spell a word like "bite" which shares a sound with "fight" but has quite a different spelling pattern.)

The first thing to establish is whether children who do not yet read can tell whether words rhyme or not. Chukovsky (1963) has collected a large corpus of anecdotal evidence which suggests that children are fascinated by rhyming words from an early age, and use them in their own language games and poems. For example, two and a half year old Tania made a poem based on the word "milk" (p.63):

Ilk-silk-tilk
I eat kasha with milk.

Ilks-silks-tilks
I eat kashas with milks.

Tania was so concerned with rhyming sounds that she invented nonsense words like "tilk" to maintain the rhyme. Dowker (1989) found that English children also make up words in order to produce rhymes in their poems. One of the examples that she gives is of three year old Afua whose poem began:

> The bird does jump,
> Mump and dump.

The experience which children get (often with the active encouragement of their parents) from rhymes such as these seems to be a natural and spontaneous part of their linguistic development. But there is systematic research which establishes beyond doubt that children can detect rhyme long before they begin to read. We shall describe two studies which do this.

The first, by Lenel and Cantor (1981), was carried out on some pre-school children with an average age of four years eleven months who had not begun to learn to read, and on five and six year old children as well. The task that Lenel and Cantor gave these children was simple. The experimenters read out one word (e.g. "pear") to them and then two other words (e.g. "chair" and "flag"). The child had to say which of these "choice words" rhymed with the first one. Sometimes the first word also shared a sound with the incorrect choice word (e.g. "sun", with the two choices "bun" and "pin").

1. Same/different judgements (Lenel & Cantor, 1971)

Target	Test pair		
	Correct	Distractor	Features of distractor
bed	sled	ring	no shared phonemes
toes	nose	tent	shared onset
drum	thumb	cup	shared vowel
sun	gun	pin	shared final consonant
mouse	house	mouth	shared CV
pan	can	pen	differ by vowel only

2. The oddity task (Bradley & Bryant, 1983)

Middle sound different					Last sound different			
mop	hop	*tap*	lop		*fan*	cat	hat	mat
pat	bat	*fit*	cat		leg	peg	*hen*	beg
lot	cot	pot	*hat*		pin	win	*sit*	fin
fun	*pin*	bun	gun		*doll*	hop	top	pop
hug	dig	pig	wig		bun	*hut*	gun	sun

FIG. 1.6.   Different measures of rhyming.

The children did quite well. The older children managed the tasks better, but the scores of the pre-school children were always well above chance level. On the whole the children made more mistakes when the incorrect choices shared some sounds with the first word, but even so the youngest groups' performance was always well above chance level.

The second study on rhyme that we shall describe, the longitudinal project carried out by Bradley and Bryant (1983), led to the same conclusion as Lenel and Cantor's had done, but on the basis of the scores of a far larger number of children. This study dealt with alliteration as well as with rhyme. The project lasted for four years and at its outset involved 403 children aged four and five years. None of these children showed any sign of reading when they were first tested; indeed over 100 other children had been eliminated from the project because they were able to read some words.

At the beginning of the project all the children were given rhyme and alliteration oddity tests. These were almost identical to the oddity tests that we described when we dealt with the Kirtley et al. study. The experimenter said three or four words at a time, and all but one of these words had a particular sound in common ("pin", "win","sit", "fin")(Fig.1.6). The child had to spot the odd word. There were three oddity tasks. In one, as in the example just described, the distinctive sound was the last consonant. In another ("lot", "cot", "pot", "hat") it was the middle, vowel sound, and in the third ("ham", "tap", "had", "hat") it was the opening consonant. The first two examples are of rhyme oddity tasks and the last is of an alliteration oddity task.

The children, pre-readers all, managed the three tasks with relative ease. There was considerable variation among the different children, but their overall performance was well above chance level. We can be certain that children can detect rhyme and alliteration before they begin to read.

THE ORIGINS OF RHYMING

The strength of this skill raises another question. How does it come about? There is a range of possibilities. At one extreme the strength of the skill could be decided genetically. The opposite extreme is that the child's home environment entirely determines how sensitive to rhyme she becomes. The truth almost certainly lies somewhere between these two. The evidence suggests that heredity and the environment both play a part, and this almost certainly means that there is an interaction between the child's genetic predispositions and the phonological experiences that she has as she grows up.

Olson, Wise, Connors and Rack (in press) looked at a large group of identical and fraternal twins, selecting twin pairs on the basis that at least one of the two was dyslexic. They gave these twins several different tests. One of these was a test of rhyme "fluency". The children were given one minute to produce as many words as they could which rhymed with "eel". There were definite signs that success in these tests was heavily influenced by the children's genetic make-up. The dyslexic children were generally rather bad at it (this as we shall see (Chapter 5) is a common result) but the important discovery was that the identical twins were more like each other than the fraternal twins were. When one identical twin was dyslexic and poor on the rhyme test, the other twin tended to manage badly in it as well. Olson et al. concluded that the dyslexic children's insensitivity to rhyme was influenced by genetic factors.

We shall have more to say about this study in later chapters when we discuss the possibility of a phonological deficit among dyslexic children. For the moment we shall deal only with the possibility raised by the Olson et al. study that rhyming skills are influenced by heredity. The results certainly point in that direction, but it is important to bear in mind that this was a study about dyslexia. What may be true of pairs of twins which include a dyslexic child may not apply to the population at large. We need another twin study, this time with good and poor readers and good and poor rhymers, to establish whether performance in rhyme tests is genetically influenced or not. One extra advantage of such a study is that it could be done with pre-readers as well as with those who have been taught, with varying degrees of success, to read.

The second study is described in two papers (MacLean, Bryant & Bradley, 1987; Bryant, Bradley, MacLean & Crossland, 1989). It suggests a way in which the child's environment may play a part. The idea that the child's parents or brothers and sisters might influence her awareness of rhyme does not on the face of it seem all that far-fetched. Parents sing songs and recite poems and nursery rhymes to their children. It is quite possible that this sort of experience could affect children's awareness of rhyme. The study in question showed that there may be a causal connection here. The authors looked at the extent of children's knowledge of common nursery rhymes among a group of 65 three and a quarter year old children, and then over the next two years measured the same children's developing sensitivity to rhyme. The measure for this was a version of the oddity test used in the Bradley and Bryant study which we have just described.

There was a connection between these two variables. The children's knowledge of nursery rhymes was strongly related to their sensitivity to rhyme two years later. This relationship held even after the differences in IQ and in the educational level of their mothers were partialled out in a multiple regression. The connection between what a child knows about nursery rhymes and her sensitivity to rhyme suggests an environmental effect. Nursery rhymes are cultural phenomena, and it is reasonable to assume that these children's familiarity with these rhymes was heavily influenced by their parents. Of course, one cannot conclude from this that the parents definitely did influence children's phonological awareness in this way, because there are other possible explanations. There may, for example, be some underlying skill which affects both the children's success with nursery rhymes and their ability to detect and analyse rhyme. But the connection is an intriguing one, and invites further investigation.

CONCLUSIONS

1. Awareness of Phonemes

The work that we have reviewed in this chapter makes us think it most unlikely that the progress that children make in reading is determined by their sensitivity to phonemes. On the contrary their progress in learning to read (or to read an alphabetic script at any rate) is probably the most important cause of awareness of phonemes. Children are not particularly sensitive to the existence of phonemes in words at the time when they begin to learn to read, and if they do not learn an alphabetic script they continue to be insensitive to these phonological units for some time.

2. Awareness of Onset and Rime

Children's phonological judgements are strongly influenced by the division between onset and rime. They can easily judge whether words have the same onset and whether they have the same rime, and these are judgements that they can make some time before they learn to read. In fact it is only after they have begun to read (though very soon after) that they begin to break these intra-syllabic units into smaller segments.

This leaves us with two questions. One is whether the awareness of intra-syllabic units which comes before learning to read does play a causal role in children's success in reading. The answer, of course, depends on empirical research, and we will be describing this in later chapters. At this stage, however, we can at least say that such a causal connection is quite a likely one. This form of awareness, as we have seen, is linked to children's skill with rhyme and alliteration, and these are activities in which children categorise words by common sounds. It seems a reasonable idea that these categories might play a significant role in learning to read and to spell. There are also groups of words which share common spelling patterns, and these are often rhyming words. So the two types of category often coincide, and that is why experience with one kind of category could help children to form the other.

So we are suggesting that there is a form of phonological analysis in reading and spelling which is quite different from the application of letter-sound rules. These rules, often referred to as grapheme-phoneme correspondence rules, link single letters or digraphs with single phonemes, and when they are used it is to construct words on a letter-by-letter basis ("shop" from "sh", "o", "p"). No doubt these rules do play a part in reading, but we suggest that there are other rules of a phonological type which are also important. The groups of written words which share a common sound as well as a common spelling pattern typically are linked by common sounds which consist of more than one phoneme, and common spelling patterns which consist of several letters ("light", "fight", "might"). Once this is recognised, it is easy to see why there should be a connection between the pre-reading phonological skills that we have described and the development of reading.

English is a capricious orthography in general, but it is much less predictable at the level of the single letter than of groups of letters. Thus a word like "light" cannot be easily read letter-by-letter, because the individual letters represent sounds which do not add up to the word "light". But it is quite possible that a child could come to read this word by learning that there is a group of written words which end in the letters "-ight", and which always end in the same rhyming sound. Mention of the vagaries of the English orthography takes us to the subject matter of the next chapter. There we will consider how children read words like "cat", which plainly fit in with a phonological code, and others like "choir", which plainly do not.

CHAPTER 2

How Children Read Words

DIFFERENT WAYS TO READ A WORD

We shall consider now what happens while young children are actually in the process of reading. Do they use their knowledge of sounds in order to read words? Do they convert letters into sounds and then work out that these sounds add up to a particular word?

The two causal notions that we discussed in Chapter 1 lead to quite different answers to this question. If the first of the two hypotheses (reading causes phonological awareness) is right, we could not expect young children who are just beginning to learn to read to use a phonological code at the very beginning stages of reading. According to this hypothesis phonological awareness must follow reading: therefore children should not be able to detect phonological segments when they first start to read. They must begin by reading in some other way.

But the other hypothesis (phonological awareness causes reading) suggests something different. If children are sensitive to sounds before they begin reading and this sensitivity affects the way that they read, they will probably take advantage of the phonological code as soon as they begin to learn to read. Of course, it is always possible that children depend on phonological skills in order to learn how to read, but do not use these skills when they are actually reading, but this seems unlikely to us. At any rate evidence that children do apply a phonological code in order to read right from the start would tell us a great deal about the role of phonological skills in learning to read.

So we have to consider whether children read words phonologically or, as we said just now, "in some other way". But what does reading "phonologically" mean? And what "other way" is there?

The phonological option is reasonably simple: children may read words by converting letters into sounds. But, given what we said in the last chapter, there are at least two possible phonological codes. One would work through *grapheme-phoneme relations*. Children using it would decipher the word "string" first by converting each of its six letters into a sound and then by putting these six sounds together.

The second possible phonological code depends on *intra-syllabic units*, onset and rime. Children who use this version of the phonological code would read "string" by recognising that "str-" represents a particular opening sound and "ing" a particular end sound and then combining these two sounds.

How useful could these two versions of the phonological code be? The answer is that although one could read many English words with the help of letter-sound relationships, one could not read them all. The English script is too unpredictable for that. The use of grapheme-phoneme relations, as we remarked at the end of Chapter 1, is particularly risky. There is a large number of English words that we cannot read by simply translating each of their individual letters into sounds. Many of these are common words and children have to learn to read them quite early on. Most children will be able to read the words "one" and "laugh", for example, after a short time at school, and yet these are words which cannot be read on a simple letter by letter basis. There has to be another way of reading.

One of these is often called the *visual strategy*, but we prefer to call it the *global strategy*. Several people have argued that one can learn to recognise particular familiar words as visual patterns. Children see written words like "school" over and over again: it seems quite a reasonable idea that these words will eventually become distinctive and easily recognisable patterns to them.

To read words as wholes without paying attention to the individual letters is, to all intents and purposes, to read in the same way as the Japanese read kanji characters. You recognise that a visual pattern signifies a particular word just as the Japanese recognise that a particular kanji character means a word. But the analogy with a logographic script like kanji helps us to see the limitations of using the visual or "logographic" strategy, as it is sometimes called, to read English. Kanji logographic characters are distinctive visual patterns: written English words are not. The shape of words, the "word envelope", is not always a good cue to distinguish between words: "cat" and "ant" have the same word envelope.

That, in fact, is the reason why we prefer to talk about the "global" rather than the "visual" strategy. It is quite possible that children might respond to the word as a whole, but as a sequence of letters rather than as a distinct visual shape. They may learn that the letters "o", "n" and "e" add up to "one" without always recognising the word as a distinctive visual pattern. That seems a reasonable way to remember, for example, what the written word "Gloucester" means.

If people read some words in a non-phonological way—as indeed they must—then they may well read all words that way. But if children must use non-phonological codes, they may not even need a phonological code, even though it could work quite well with a large number of written English words. We have to look to empirical evidence to see if children do read any words phonologically. If it turns out that they do, then we shall also need to know whether the phonological code that they use works through grapheme-phoneme relations or through larger phonological units like rime and onset.

THE EVIDENCE ON THE DIFFERENT STRATEGIES

Reading without Phonology

We shall begin our description of the empirical evidence by describing some studies which show that young children do often read in a decidedly non-phonological way. The possibility of an entirely non-phonological, visual or logographic code, itself leads to an interesting and quite plausible hypothesis. Children might initially learn to read words on the basis of letter-sound relationships, and then much later they might come to recognise them as familiar wholes. Visual recognition would only become important later on because the children would have to meet the written words many times before becoming familiar enough with them to be able to recognise them as familiar patterns.

Concurrent Vocalisation

Some time ago Barron and Baron (1977) set out to investigate this two-stage hypothesis. They devised two tasks and gave them to children whose ages ranged from six years (these were children who had only just begun to learn to read) through to thirteen years. One of the two tasks was meant to be a measure of the way that children read, and the other was designed as a task in which they had to pay attention to the sounds of the words that they were reading.

In the task which was designed as a straightforward test of the children's ability to read the words (the "meaning" task), Barron and Baron showed the children five pictures, each with a written word beside it. The children had to pick out those pairs in which the picture and the word "went together". Sometimes they did, and sometimes not. One pair in which the picture and word "went together" (a correct pair) was a picture of some trousers beside the written word "shirt". It was taken for granted that the children would see the conceptual connection between shirt and trousers: Barron and Baron assumed that, as long as the children could read the written words, they would be able to work out which pairs were the correct ones and which incorrect.

The other test was a rhyme task. The children were again shown five pictures, each with a written word beside it, but this time they had to pick out the pairs in which the word rhymed with the picture's name (e.g. a pair with a picture of a horn and the word "corn"). Again the name of the object in the picture and the word beside it did rhyme in some of the pairs (the correct pairs), but not in others.

Barron and Baron gave these tasks to the children in two ways. In one condition the children did the tasks in silence: they simply marked the correct pairs without saying anything, and nothing was said to them as they did so. The other condition was not silent: while the children were marking the correct pairs, they had to repeat the word "double" out loud continuously.

The reason for imposing this extra burden—which is usually called *concurrent vocalisation*—was that it ought to interfere with any phonological judgements that the child might be making. If children have to keep saying a word out loud they should as a result find it more difficult to think about the sounds in words at the same time. In fact the experiment contained a check that the concurrent vocalisation would have this effect: if the act of saying "double, double..." does indeed get in the way of thinking about the words' constituent sounds, it ought to make the rhyme task a great deal harder.

The experimenters wanted to know if it would make the "meaning" task more difficult as well. As this task was devised as a simple test of reading, Barron and Baron argued that the amount of interference that was produced by concurrent vocalisation should be a good measure of the children's dependence on the phonological strategy.

Suppose that children initially read phonologically but later, as they gradually become familiar with the written appearance of particular words, begin to adopt the visual strategy. In that case, the effect of concurrent vocalisation should be the same in both tasks for the younger children. It should interfere equally with the rhyme and the meaning tasks as these children would depend on phonological codes in both tasks. On the other hand, among the older children concurrent vocalisation should have less effect on the "meaning" task than on the rhyme task, because these children would rely less on phonological codes in the former task (as they now recognise many of the words visually), but would still have to make phonological judgements in the rhyme task. This was the pattern that Barron and Baron expected. It was not the pattern that they found.

At every age level the children were held back in the rhyme task by concurrent vocalisation. This was to be expected: that task involved phonological judgements which a child would find it hard to make at the same time as she was repeating a word out loud.

The surprise was that concurrent vocalisation had *no* detectable effect on the meaning task at any age. The children could work out the meanings of the written words in that task as well and as quickly when they were repeating the word "double" as when they did the task in silence. So, even though concurrent vocalisation hampers children's phonological judgements, it leaves their reading unscathed. It seems a reasonable conclusion that they could read the words that they were given without having to use any phonological knowledge.

So the experiment suggests that six year old children who are no more than "beginning readers" are able to read words without the help of phonology. The idea that only children who have been reading for several years can use a non-phonological code may be wrong.

Of course, one cannot be completely sure that the experiment proves that the children were reading without the help of phonology. Another possibility is that they do read phonologically, but that they make one kind of phonological judgement when they read (which is not impaired by concurrent vocalisation), and quite a different kind in the rhyme task (which is vulnerable to concurrent vocalisation). This alternative explanation was adopted by Besner (1987), who has shown that concurrent vocalisation does not affect some judgements that adults make about written words, even though it does affect their judgements about rhyme. However, some further experiments, all of them inspired by Barron and Baron's provocative study, make this alternative idea seem implausible.

Barron and Baron had concluded that children do not usually pay attention to letter-sound relationships when they read for meaning. But there is a hidden assumption here, which is that concurrent vocalisation would impair children's performance if they were forced to pay attention to single letters of the words that they were reading. So, we need another task in which children have to respond to single letters and to the sounds that these letters represent. Bryant and Bradley (1983) attempted to fill this gap in a further experiment in which they gave six and seven year old children four different tasks.

One, the whole word task, was very like Barron and Baron's meaning task. The children were given sets of 10 pictures on one side and 10 words on the other, and they had to draw lines between each picture and the appropriate written word (between, for example, a picture of a man and the word "man"). Some of the sets of 10 words and pictures contained words which were quite easy to read, and others harder words.

The remaining tasks were single letter tasks. They were exactly the same as the whole word task, except that the written words were incomplete. The children were given 10 pictures and 10 incomplete words which consisted of one visible and two obviously scratched out letters. This made it quite clear that each visible letter was part of an incompletely written word. So, in the first letter task[1] the set might contain a picture of a man and also the incomplete word "m**". In the middle letter task the equivalent incomplete word was "*a*", and in the final letter task "**n". The children did each task under two conditions. In one condition they were silent; in the other (concurrent vocalisation) they had to say "bla, bla ..." repeatedly.

Barron and Baron had concluded that children read words without being disturbed by concurrent vocalisation because they treat the words as though they were logographs. If that is right, concurrent vocalisation should have no effect at all on the whole word task, but should hamper the children in the single letter tasks where they must pay attention to individual letters and the sounds that they represent.

That is what happened in Bryant and Bradley's experiment. When the children had to repeat the "bla, bla" incantation in the three single letter tasks they made many mistakes—many more than when they did the same tasks in silence. On the other hand, concurrent vocalisation had no effect on the way that they coped in the whole word task, whether the words that they had to read were the easy or difficult ones. This difference between the single letter tasks on the one hand and the whole word tasks on the other cannot have anything to do with the absolute difficulty of these tasks. In the silent condition the children made as many mistakes with the difficult whole words as they did in the single letter tasks. Yet concurrent vocalisation had no impact on the way that they read these difficult words, even though it made the single letter tasks so difficult. Once again concurrent vocalisation disrupted a reading task which needed phonological analysis, but had no effect on another task in which children had to read whole words.

This result makes Besner's alternative most unlikely. He, you will remember, had claimed that concurrent vocalisation holds back judgements about rhyme, but not what he called pre-lexical phonological judgements—judgements, made prior to understanding the written word, about its constituent sounds. Yet we have shown that concurrent vocalisation does impair children's decisions about the sounds of individual letters even though it has no appreciable effect on their judgements about whole words.

We conclude that even beginning readers can, and often do, read whole words without analysing the grapheme-phoneme relations in those words. They seem to take quite easily to reading words as logograms. Of course we do not claim that children never attend to the sounds that characterise the individual letters in a word. In fact, in Chapter 4, we shall show that they can use their knowledge of spelling-sound relationships, when they read, in a sophisticated way. At the moment we only suggest that the young children find it easy to take the logographic approach.

But how exactly do they do that? One possibility is that English children adopt a global (or visual) strategy. In that case one should be able to demonstrate that English children read words in much the same way as Japanese children, for example, read genuine logograms. The Japanese, it will be recalled, have two types of script. One of them, the kanji script, is logographic: each kanji character symbolises a word. In the other kind of script, called kana, each character represents a syllable: so this second script is phonological, but not "phonemic".

Kana, Kanji and the Logographic Strategy

One has to read the kanji script visually, and so concurrent vocalisation should not have any effect on children reading these characters. The children should do so as well when they have to intone a word repeatedly as when they read kanji words in silence. However, as each kanji character is a visual pattern which symbolises a whole word, it should be possible to devise a form of visual interference which would disrupt children reading this script. One way to do this would be to have pictures of objects paired with kanji words (in a Japanese version of Barron and Baron's picture-word pairs), but to have incorrect pairs which contain a kanji character which does not represent the object in the picture but looks very like the kanji that does.

Kimura and Bryant (1983) had the idea of looking at Japanese children reading kanji and kana with two types of interference—*phonological interference* (concurrent vocalisation) and *visual confusability*. They gave seven year old Japanese children sets of picture-word pairs: each pair was on a card and the children had to sort them into correct pairs, where the written word represented the object in the picture, and incorrect ones, where it did not. Sometimes the words were written in kanji, sometimes in kana (Fig.2.1).

In half the sets there was an element of visual confusability, in that the written word in each incorrect pair looked very similar to the word which did signify the object in

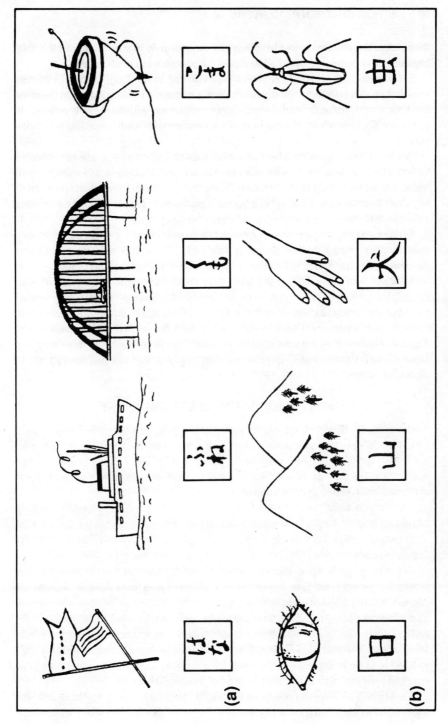

FIG. 2.1.　The interference task (Kimura & Bryant, 1983): correct and incorrect pairs. (a) Kanji-picture pairs; (b) Kana-picture pairs.

the picture. The children were also given half the sets to do in silence: in the other half (concurrent vocalisation) they had to repeat a Japanese word continuously.

Let us deal first with the children's performance in the kanji tasks. Concurrent vocalisation had no effect at all on the children's success in reading kanji. On the other hand, the visual confusability did: the children were slower with the visually confusable kanji lists. So, concurrent vocalisation did not interfere with reading that has to be done visually.

But it did hold the children back in the kana tasks. The children made their choices with the kana picture-word pairs more slowly and less accurately when they had to intone a word repeatedly than when they did the task in silence. Concurrent vocalisation impaired their attempts to decipher a phonological script. This is our first convincing evidence that children use phonological cues when they read.

Kimura and Bryant (1983) then gave the same kind of task (except that they only used English words) to English seven year olds. These children also had to sort picture-word pairs. Again, half of the lists involved visual confusability while the other half did not, and again half of the tasks were done silently and the other half with concurrent vocalisation. The pattern of the English children's scores was very similar to that of the Japanese children in the kanji tasks. Once again concurrent vocalisation had no effect: once again visual confusability held the children back considerably. English children, it now seems clear, often read English words in the same way as a Japanese child reads kanji. English children apply a logographic strategy to an alphabetic script.

The Whole Word Method

The strength of the non-phonological, global or logographic strategy and the abundant signs that children take to it easily and naturally may come as something of a surprise, but it has been almost a commonplace in educational circles for some time. It is the justification for the idea of the "whole word method" which some teachers support enthusiastically although others do not.

The "whole word" method can take many forms, but it usually entails teaching beginning readers to recognise words as complete units rather than to use letter-sound associations. The fact that some children are taught in this way gives us another way of seeing whether some children can read without the help of phonological rules.

Some time ago Alegria, Pignot and Morais (1982) showed that children who are taught in this way are less successful in tasks in which they have to manipulate phonemes than children taught in the more normal "phonic" manner. They worked with a group of six year old children whose teachers had used the whole word method only and had given the children no instruction about phonemes whatsoever. They gave them two kinds of "reversal" task. In one, the children heard a two-phoneme word like "os", and had to say it backwards. In the other, the word that they heard was a two-syllable one, and their task was to reverse the order of those syllables.

These children were as good as others taught "phonically" in the syllable task, but a great deal worse when it came to reversing phonemes. So children who are not taught about phonemes are fairly insensitive to them. How does this affect the way that they read?

Seymour and Elder (1986) tried to answer this question. They looked at a class of primary school children who were taught over their first year by the whole word method. Seymour and Elder were particularly interested in the kind of mistakes that these children made in reading words, and concluded that most of the mistakes showed that the children read words as logograms.

The most striking examples were the words which they read as completely different words with no phonological relation to the written word in front of them, but with a similar meaning to the correct word. So, for example, they would read "white" as "green", "children" as "girl", "lions" as "tigers", and "car" as "wheels". Seymour and Elder argued that these mistakes showed that the children paid little attention to letter-sound relationships when reading, and simply associated the whole word with a particular meaning though not always with precisely the right meaning.

Seymour and Elder also report that the children made very few errors which could be described as phonological. There were hardly any instances of children misreading a word using letter-sound rules. For example, they rarely created new words like "wass" for "was", or read "of" as "off". Another extremely interesting observation that these authors made was that these children tended to be flummoxed by completely new words. This should remind us of a major difference between a phonological and a logographic strategy. The logographic strategy simply involves the recognition of words that are already familiar ones, and gives you no way to work out the meaning of a new word without the help of someone who knows what it means. But with a phonological strategy one can in principle work out the meaning of completely unfamiliar words, provided that the sound of the word when it is spoken is reasonably well related to the typical sounds of the letters in the written word. We shall return to this theme in Chapter 4.

Seymour and Elder's interesting study had one main weakness. They made no comparisons with other children who had been taught, as most children are taught, about letter-sound relationships as well as about whole words. So we do not know whether the striking signs of a strong visual strategy that Seymour and Elder found in their whole word group would also appear among children who have been taught in a different way. It is an interesting question, and worth pursuing.

Comparisons between Strategies

There are other ways of looking at the strength of the different strategies in children's reading. Snowling and Frith (1981) devised one of the most ingenious of these. They pointed out that it is possible to distort the visual appearance of script and yet keep its phonological aspects unchanged and vice versa, and they wondered which kind of distortion would have the greater effect. Obviously, if children read visually they will be most affected by a script that looks unusual (RoBiN, for example), and if they read phonologically they will be held back if the letters in the words do not represent the right sounds even if the word's appearance has not changed much.

Snowling and Frith used three kinds of distortion, which made their experiment a fairly complex one. They gave seven year old children who were either good or poor readers three types of sentences to read. The sentences were either: (1) phonologically meaningful but orthographically distorted ("Mothur gaiv Tom a redd bocks"); (2) written in script which visually approximated real words ("..lookcd in tho bcx fcr hjs tcys..."), even though both orthographic and phonological information was distorted; or (3) visually distorted but with letter conjunction and phonology preserved ("a RoBln HopPed uP to MY wiNdow") (see Fig.2.2).

The experimenters measured the time that it took children to read the three kinds of sentence, and compared these times with the time taken to read sentences presented in normal script. There was a difference between the children who were good at reading and those who were not. The good readers were hardly affected by the script in which the right sequence of letters was preserved even though visual cues were affected ("a RoBln HopPed uP to MY wiNdow"). But they were slowed appreciably by the two other types of distortion, in which the sequence of letters was definitely not right ("Mothur gaiv Tom a redd bocks"), and "...lookcd in tho bcx fcr hjs"). So the sequences of letters, and not the words' visual appearance or the sounds produced by grapheme-phoneme relations, are important to these children.

The effects were rather different on the weaker readers. They were held back by all three distortions, but they were particularly poor when they tried to work out the sentences which could only be read with the help of grapheme-phoneme rules ("Mothur gaiv Tom a redd bocks"). Thus the most striking feature of their performance seemed to be that they found it hard to use letter-sound relationships in order to decipher these strange words.

The fact that the children who had made the least progress in reading were the ones who were most thrown off track by having to read the phonological script supports the

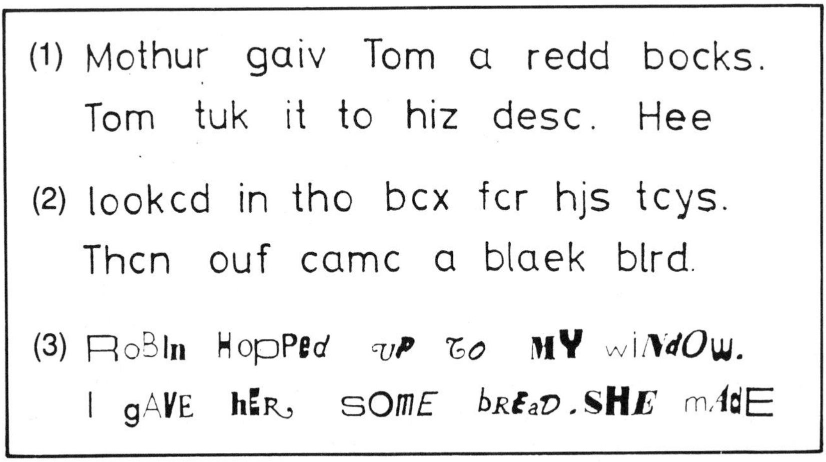

FIG. 2.2.   The distorted text task (Snowling & Frith, 1981). (Reproduced with permission from the *British Journal of Psychology, 72*, 85.)

idea that early reading is not phonological. Snowling and Frith's conclusion[2] that "...the results add little weight to any argument which suggests that it is necessary for children to decode letters to sound before understanding meaning" (1981, p. 87) seems quite reasonable.

Arguments for Phonological Reading

Can it be that children's awareness of sounds plays no part in their reading? All the studies that we have reviewed so far seem to point in that direction. But a flat conclusion that grapheme-phoneme correspondences are after all unnecessary still seems quite implausible to us. For one thing, the evidence from studies on illiterate people and on comparisons of people who read alphabetic scripts and those who do not (reviewed in the first chapter) suggests a connection between our awareness of phonemes and our knowledge of the alphabetic system. For another, in principle, it seems unlikely that the alphabet should have been invented and used so widely if its basic feature, the relation between single letters and single phonemes, plays no part. If children read words as logograms, why not just give them logograms to read? Wouldn't it be more convenient not to have to bother with strings of letters and to represent each word by a pattern?

There is another possibility—that the experiments that we have described so far force the children to read in an uncharacteristic and unrepresentative way. In that case more sensitive experiments, designed especially to pick up signs of phonological activities, should show that children do use letter-sound relationships when they read.

Regularity and Irregularity

There is one good thing at least to be said about the caprices of English spelling. They are a great help to people who are trying to work out whether children depend on a phonological code in order to read. If children adopt, say, a purely visual code to read, the fact that the same sequences of letters represent quite different sounds in different words ("gave", "have") should not bother them at all. In that case, each word will simply be a distinctive visual pattern to them and there is no reason why irregular words should be any more distinctive than regular ones. So, if children read in a visual way, regular and irregular words should be equally easy for them. But if they depend on letter-sound relationships, they will read regular words more easily than irregular ones.

But what exactly is the difference between regular and irregular? In a regular word, the sounds are written in a regular way. The sequence of letters in the words represent sounds in the same way as the same sequences do in other words. The word "sing" is regular: we call it regular because it is spelled in an entirely orthodox manner. Most words which end with the letters "-ing" rhyme with "sing" and most words which start as "sing" does also begin with the same sound as it.

(Notice that we concentrated on this word's onset and rime. In fact one can discuss regularity and irregularity at the level of the phoneme too, but then one opens the door for much more inconsistency. The letters "ing" almost invariably signify the sound which is the rime in "sing". But the letter "i" represents different phonemes in different words ("in", "find"). In fact it seems to us that there has not been enough discussion of the nature of the sounds that we are dealing with when we distinguish regular from irregular words. But this is an aside.)

We are now in a position to consider what an irregular word is. There are two main kinds of irregular words as far as reading is concerned. These are "exception" words, and "ambiguous" words. An exception word contains a sequence of letters which in other words means one sound, but in this particular word means a completely different sound. "Have" and "said" are examples. "Have" is an exception because the letters "-ave" usually add up to the end sound (the rime) that one finds in words like "gave" and "save". "Said" is untypical because the letters "-aid" usually signify the rime in "maid" and "raid". So "gave" and "maid" contain the sounds usually associated with this letter sequence, and "have" and "said" do not.

Ambiguous words are not the same. They too contain sequences of letters which signify different sounds in different words. But here there are no clear regular and exception words. Words which end in the letters "-own" are an example. Sometimes the letters represent one sound ("clown"), sometimes another ("blown"), and there is no reason for saying that one set of words is the rule, the other the exception.

If (as we have noted) children use a phonological code of some sort to help them read, they should make more mistakes when they come across irregular words, and so they should be less successful with exception words and with ambiguous words than with regular words. But before turning to the data we should note briefly that sometimes people define regularity in a way that is different from ours. Sometimes, people describe a written word as regular when its letters represent the phonemes in that word. So "bed" according to this definition is highly regular and "laugh" quite irregular. In practice, there is not all that much difference between this approach and the one that we have adopted, because on the whole regular words are regular in both schemes. But this second way of looking at regularity misses the inconsistency associated with ambiguous words, and that as we shall see is important. The second definition may also give spurious support to the importance of phonemes. At any rate, we shall stick as closely as we can to the first definition of regularity. Let us look at the data.

We shall describe two kinds of experiment on the effects of irregularity. In one, children are simply asked to read regular and irregular words. The other kind of study involves the "lexical decision" method: children have to make judgements about whether the words that they see are real words or not: only some of these words are real ones, and while some are regular, others are not.

There are many examples of the first type of study. The most important, almost certainly, is the experiment by Backman, Bruck, Hebert and Seidenberg (1984), because they included ambiguous as well as exception words in the lists that they gave children to read. These children's ages ranged from seven to nine years. The children made more mistakes when trying to read the exception and the ambiguous words than they did with the regular words. So, both kinds of irregularity do make it harder for children to read, and this must mean that they are to some extent dependent on letter-sound relationships when they read. But we say "to some extent" deliberately, because it may have been to a very small extent. The fact is that the differences between children's scores in the three lists were very small.

The differences were small too, and this time not even statistically significant, in a study by V. Coltheart, Laxon, Keating and Pool (1986). These authors asked some nine year old children to read a list of regular words and another of irregular words (the irregular words seem all to have been exception words, such as "break", "pint" and "come"). The children made more mistakes with the irregular list, but not many more. In this study each of the lists contained 20 words, and the children managed on average to get 16.11 of them right in the regular list and 15.8 in the irregular list—an insignificant and a non-significant difference.

So there are some signs of what is often called the "regularity effect" in children, but it seems to be pretty puny. Lexical decision tasks do not add much to our confidence in the importance of the effect in children's reading. Coltheart and her colleagues asked the same nine year old children to sort cards with regular words, irregular words (again exception words) and nonsense words on them into two piles, one of real words and the other of words that did not make sense. The children did misplace some of the real words, but no more of these mistakes involved irregular than regular words. So there was no regularity effect in this lexical decision task. And there was only a relatively small effect in an experiment conducted by Barron (1980) with much older children. He gave 12 year old children whom he divided into good and not so good readers a different form of the lexical decision task. The children were shown words one by one and had to judge whether each was a real word or not, but in this case the main measure was of the time that they took to make each decision. The real words were either regular or irregular (exception) words. Barron found a small but definite regularity effect among the good readers: these children were quicker to judge regular words as real ones and slower to do so with irregular words. But there was no difference among the poorer readers. Barron concluded that the more advanced readers did attend to sounds when they read the words that he gave them, but that the others did not.

The strongest evidence that we have to date for a regularity effect comes from a study by Schlapp and Underwood (1988) with 10 year old children. These experimenters set out to repeat Barron's results, and at the same time to look at a group of children whose spelling was poor even though their reading had reached a satisfactory level, as well as at a group of poor readers and another group who read and spelled well. The experimenters found a fairly strong regularity effect in the two groups of children who read well (Good Readers/Good Spellers and Good Readers/Poor Spellers), but there was no sign of the effect in the group of children whose reading was poor.

The search for a regularity effect has in the end provided some, albeit rather inconsistent, signs that children use a phonological code when they read. The evidence that we have looked at certainly does not suggest that this code plays a significant role in young children's reading. But there is something there, at any rate with children who have been reading for four or five years and have made satisfactory progress in reading.

There is, however, another uncertainty about the regularity effect and this is directly relevant to one of the main themes of this book. We cannot be sure what level of phonological unit is demonstrated by the regularity effect when it does occur. Does the effect (if it is found) show that children use grapheme-phoneme correspondences? Or are children concentrating on other speech units, like onset and rime? Psychologists often write as though the effect demonstrates that people are using grapheme-phoneme rules, but this need not be so. It is quite possible to describe the difference between regular and irregular words in terms of the relations between letter sequences and onset and rime units.

Let us take as an example the first few words in Barron's lists of regular and irregular words. The regular words are "fact", "pine", "list", "deal", "drum", and "held". In each of these, the sequence of letters that represents the word's rime consistently signifies the same rime in other words as well ("tact" "wine" etc.). But we do not find the same consistency when we look at the spelling of the rime in Barron's irregular words. In that sense the spelling sequence in the words "none", "lose", "love", "half", "pier", and "sign" are all inconsistent. The letter sequence that indicates the rime in each of the irregular words has a different significance elsewhere ("bone", "rose", "move"). So the fairly small regularity effect that has been found may have nothing to do with phonemes. The regularity effect may mean that children learn connections between onsets and rimes and sequences of letters.

Decisions about Sentences

There is one well-known study which is often used as evidence for the importance of the phonological code in children's reading. It was devised by Doctor and M. Coltheart (1980). They argued that the sounds of the words that a person is reading should play no part at all if the person reads visually. If you read a word as a visual pattern, they claimed, that pattern takes you directly to the word's meaning. You do not have to bother with the word's sounds. So, according to this argument, if children do in some way pay attention to the sounds of the words that they are reading they must be doing more than just recognising the words as familiar visual patterns.

In this study children had to read sentences and to decide whether or not these were meaningful. Some of the sentences made perfect sense, but others did not. Some of the meaningless sentences sounded meaningful (e.g. "She blue up the balloon"). Others were simply meaningless from both points of view: the sentence made no sense and nor did the sounds (e.g. "She know up the balloon"). Some of the sentences contained nonsense words as well as real ones (e.g. "I have noe time" and "I have bloo time"). Doctor and Coltheart argued that if the children attend to the sounds of the words, it would be much harder for them to realise that a sentence was wrong when they were given the first kind of meaningless sentence (sounds correct) than when they read the second (sounds silly). On the other hand, if the children simply read by translating visual patterns into meaning there should be no difference between the two (Fig.2.3).

Real words			
BLUE, KNOW	*Decision*	*BLEW, NO*	*Decision*
The sky is big.	YES	She picks up the balloon.	YES
The sky is blue.	YES	She blew up the balloon.	YES
The sky is blew.	NO	She blue up the balloon.	NO
I have blue time.	NO	I blew your name.	NO
The sky is no.	NO	She know up the balloon.	NO
I have know time.	NO	I no your name.	NO
I have no time.	YES	I know your name.	YES

Nonsense words			
The sky is bloo.	NO	She bloo up the balloon.	NO
The sky is noe.	NO	She noe up the balloon.	NO
I have bloo time.	NO	I bloo your name.	NO
I have noe time.	NO	I noe your name.	NO

FIG. 2.3.   The sentence comprehension task (Doctor & M. Coltheart, 1980).

The children who took part were aged between six and 10 years. Doctor and Coltheart believed that phonological codes are most prevalent early on in learning to read. So they expected that young children would find it harder than older children to reject the meaningless sentences which sounded correct.

That was what they did find. All the children were worse at rejecting meaningless sentences whose sounds made sense than sentences which sounded nonsensical. But the difference was far greater in the younger children who had just begun to learn to read. They were nearly as accurate as the older children at rejecting the sentences that sounded nonsensical, but were far worse than these older children with the sentences that sounded correct.

Doctor and Coltheart concluded from this that the phonological strategy does play a part in children's reading and particularly in young children's reading. This of course is a radically different conclusion from the one reached by Barron and Baron, Bryant and Bradley or Snowling and Frith. Did Doctor and Coltheart manage to detect phonological activities which were not noticed in other experiments?

In fact it seems to us that Doctor and Coltheart's study did not really establish that young children read words on the basis of letter-sound relationships. If you read in this way, you start with the letters and sounds, put the sounds together and decide what the word means. The phonological activity is "pre-lexical", to use an unnecessarily technical term. But the "sounds" with which Doctor and Coltheart are concerned come after the word has been deciphered—they are "post-lexical". The results of their study certainly establish that sounds are involved in children's reading somewhere, but there is nothing to show that children pay any attention to letters and sounds before they have actually read the word. The children may have recognised the written word "blue" as a visual pattern which is associated with the sound "bloo". So they may have accepted sentences like "She blue up the balloon" as meaningful because they knew that "blue" was a meaningful word, but did not know that "blue" was the incorrect spelling of the word "blew".

This interpretation is supported by the fact that even the six year olds accepted significantly fewer of the sentences involving nonsense words as meaningful even if they sounded correct. It seems likely that they knew that "bloo" was a funny way of spelling "blew" because they had never seen it before, whereas when the comparison was between "blew" and "blue" they were on more shaky ground.

The Effect of a Phonological Prompt

So we should look for evidence of pre-lexical phonological activity. At least one psychologist has tried to provide this. Reitsma (1984) argued that if beginning readers depend on letter-sound relationships to read words, then they should be helped by being given cues about the sounds of the words that they are trying to read. He tested this by asking children aged from seven to twelve years to make such decisions about the meaning of a written word when they were given appropriate or misleading cues about the sounds of that word.

The job that the children were given was to decide whether a written word fitted in with something that they had just been told. To take two examples, they were told "This is an animal", and were then shown the printed word "bunny", or they were told "This happens sometimes in the street", and the word that followed was also "bunny". In both cases they had to say whether the sentence described the written word properly, and so the answer was "Yes" in the first example and "No" in the second.

Before they actually saw the printed words the children were given an "auditory" cue. They were asked to repeat a sound. Sometimes this sound represented a sound in the written word, and thus was appropriate: at other times it did not. So if the written word was "bunny", an appropriate cue would be the sound "bu" and an inappropriate one the sound "lu". The children had to repeat the sound that they were given as a cue over and over again (a form of concurrent vocalisation) while they tried to decide whether the written word confirmed the auditory proposition or not.

Reitsma found that the seven year old children were much slower at reaching a decision when the sound that they had been given as a cue was an inappropriate one ("lu" for "bunny"). But he did not find this difference between the effects of the appropriate and the inappropriate auditory cue in any of the older groups. In another experiment he found the same difference in the effect of the two kinds of cue in seven year old children even when they did not have to repeat the sound in question.

Reitsma concluded that he had shown that young children—beginning readers—do have to pay attention to the word's constituent sounds in order to be able to work out what a word means. But it is difficult to agree wholeheartedly, because there are other ways of explaining this result. One is that it is not really clear that the children were being helped by the appropriate cue: they may have been hindered by both, but hindered less by the appropriate cue than by the inappropriate cue.

There is a second and, in our view, more serious objection. The effect—the difference between the two kinds of cue—may have had nothing to do with the way children read normally. To show that children find it easier to recognise a word if they are told one of its sounds does not mean that they attend to these sounds when they read normally. They have simply been given an extra, singularly unusual, cue and apparently they take advantage of it. But that does not tell us how they read when, as usual, that cue is not available to them.

The Mistakes that Children make when Reading

Doctor and Coltheart's, and Reitsma's attempts to demonstrate the importance of the phonological code have failed in the end to convince us that children do read words by translating their letters into sounds, and it is hard to find any other published paper that does provide any reasonable support for the phonological connection. Recently, however, two Austrian psychologists mounted an interesting attack on the idea that young children begin by reading words in a logographic way: the report of their study is not published yet (Wimmer & Hummer, 1989).

They worked with a group of seven year old children who had just begun to learn to read. They asked these children to read a set of words some of which were real words and others nonsense words (words like "Mama" (Mummy), "Mana" (nonsense), "Auto" (car) and "Eufo" (nonsense)). Most of Wimmer and Hummer's argument is based on the mistakes that the children made when they read these words. We shall take their mistakes with the real words first. Unlike the children in the group studied by Seymour and Elder (1986), these children seemed to take account of the sounds represented by at least some of the words' letters when they went wrong. Most of their mistakes took the form of them producing a nonsense word instead of a correct meaningful word: the nonsense word usually began with the same letter as the correct word, and thus was "at least partially phonologically correct".

This is an impressive result. For one thing it suggests that Seymour and Elder's very different data can be entirely explained by the fact that the Scottish group had been taught to read words as wholes. The Scottish children probably read words as logograms because they were taught to do so. But, of course, we cannot be sure of this because there are so many other differences between the children in the two studies. One group was Scottish, for example, and the other Austrian. At the very least Wimmer and Hummer's results remind us that there is an urgent need to repeat the Seymour and Elder study with a control group of children who are being taught to read using phonic methods.

But the most important consequence of Wimmer and Hummer's discovery of non-logographic mistakes is that it definitely does show that these children made phonological judgements of a sort when trying to read words—or at any rate when they were trying to read words which they could not recognise as familiar patterns. We can conclude that these children did use the phonological strategy with words which they could not read, though we cannot assume from this that they use the same strategy with words which they know how to read already.

However, this does not necessarily mean that the phonological strategy which they adopt depends on single grapheme-phoneme correspondences. Remember that the phonological similarity between the correct word and the wrong word which they produced tended to take the form of both words beginning with the same sound. In most cases, therefore, the correct and the incorrect word must have had the same onset. So the children's phonological strategy may have been based on onset (and possibly on rime too) rather than on phonemes. We cannot tell yet: we still need more analyses of the type that Wimmer and Hummer (1989) have made, and those analyses would have to concentrate on words which have more than one phoneme as an onset (e.g. "string"), in comparison to words with single-phoneme onsets (e.g. "sing").

We do have one small caveat about the result that we have just been discussing. In the lists that Wimmer and Hummer gave the children to read, nonsense words rubbed shoulders with real words, and the children knew that this was so. This could have had the effect of making them more willing to pronounce a word which they did not recognise as a nonsense word, and in fact it could have encouraged them to adopt the phonological strategy. After all, nonsense words cannot be recognised as visual wholes, because they are by definition unfamiliar. Therefore, the children had to adopt a phonological strategy (though not necessarily a grapheme-phoneme strategy) to read nonsense words, and that may have encouraged them to adopt the same strategy with all the words that they were unable to recognise. That would have been the sensible thing for them to do,[3] since they had no way of telling whether such words were nonsense words or not.

The reason for including nonsense words was that they cannot be read logographically and therefore are a test of children's ability to adopt a phonological strategy. Wimmer and Hummer report that the children could read nonsense words quite well, and also were reasonably successful at spelling them. However, that does not mean that these children necessarily read real words in the same way.

CONCLUSIONS

In this chapter we have had to come to two uncomfortable conclusions —uncomfortable, at any rate, for the authors of a book about phonological awareness and reading. The first is that there is very little direct evidence that children who are learning to read do rely on letter-sound relationships to help them read words. The second is that there is a great deal of evidence that these young children take easily and naturally to reading words in other ways: they adopt a global strategy, which means that they either recognise the word as a pattern or remember it as a sequence of letters.

We have two pressing reasons for not shutting up shop at this point. One is that children do not just read written language: they produce it as well, and to do so they have to learn how to spell. As we shall see in the next chapter, the experimental evidence on spelling makes a stark contrast to the equivalent data on children's reading. Children do depend heavily on letter-sound relations when they write words.

Another reason for continuing the quest for the connection which has proved so hard to detect in the work reviewed in this chapter is that most of that work has been based on the idea that a phonological code works through grapheme-phoneme correspondences. But we have already seen that there are other speech units to think about than the phoneme. Onset and rime are easily available to young children, and there are strong and consistent relations between these units and sequences of letters, like "str-", "qu-", "-ight", "-and" and "-ing". In Chapter 4 we shall describe experimental evidence that shows that this type of connection between phonological units and strings of letters plays a considerable part in children's reading.

NOTES

1.   Besner (1987) wrongly called these judgements "rhyming judgements involving ... a letter and a picture" (p. 471). He was wrong because the sounds associated with the letters did not rhyme with the names of the pictures. "n" does not rhyme with man, and so to work out that **n goes with the picture of a man is not a rhyming judgement.

2.   Snowling and Frith (1981) called the first kind of distortion P (phonologically similar), and argued that it should not affect children who were reading phonologically. They called the second kind V (visually similar), and suggested that it should have no effect on children who read visually (in terms of global visual recognition strategies). Their label for the third script which preserved the letter sequences and the phonological relations was M (mixed script).

They were interested in isolating the effects of phonological, orthographic, and shape (visual) cues in reading. They argued that by subtracting the time taken to read the normal (N) sentences from the three separate kinds of distortion, the effects due to the reduction of these cues could be calculated. The effect of reducing orthographic cues could be estimated from (P-N)-(M-N), while the effect of reducing sound cues could be estimated from (V-N)- (P-N-(M-N)). They reasoned that if the effect of the multiple distortion ("a RoBin"), which reduced shape cues, was subtracted from the effects of the phonetic distortion ("redd bocks"), which reduced orthographic and shape cues, then the effect due to orthographic distortion alone could be derived. Similarly, if this orthographic distortion was then subtracted from the effects of the visual distortion ("hjs tcys"), which reduced orthographic and sound cues, then the effect due to phonetic distortion alone could be derived. From this, Snowling and Frith showed that the good readers were disturbed most by the reduction of orthographic cues, while reduction of each of the cues had much the same effect as each other on the poor readers.

This reasoning is not completely convincing. It is based on the questionable assumption that the distortion of the shape cues in the phonological ("redd bocks") and multiple ("a RoBIn") scripts are equivalent. But the two kinds of distortion are visually very dissimilar, and so we cannot be sure about Snowling and Frith's elaborate equations. The straightforward comparison of the relative difficulty of reading the three kinds of distorted text seems the interesting one to us.

3.   In the next chapter we shall report a study (Bryant & Bradley, 1980), which shows that children definitely do adopt a phonological strategy if they are asked to read lists which contain both real and nonsense words.

CHAPTER 3

Spelling and Phonological Awareness

INVENTED SPELLING

A six year old English girl began a story that she was writing about a burglary with the sentence "Tom nicta cr" (meaning "Tom nicked a car"). Her spelling, although attractive, was not perfect, but the mistakes that she made tell us a great deal. These are orthographic mistakes, but it would be churlish to call them phonological errors, because the girl actually managed to preserve the phonological relations between the letters and the sound of the words that she was trying to produce very well.

"Nicta" is a better phonological representation of the sounds of the words "nicked a" than is the traditional spelling. It happens that we tend to write the end of past verbs with "-ed" and no doubt there are good reasons for doing so. Nevertheless, the final consonant in these verbs is often a "t" sound , and that is presumably why the girl wrote the letter "t" rather than "d" or "ed". Even her two-letter version of "car" is probably a misguided attempt to get the sound of that word across properly. Young children often confuse the names of letters with the sounds, and of course the letter name "R" corresponds exactly with the sound of the last two phonemes (with the rime, in fact) in "car".

This girl, a beginning reader and a beginning speller, was plainly paying considerable attention to the relationship between letters and sounds in the words that she was writing. She is no exception. It was Charles Read (1971, 1975) who first pointed out the significance, as well as the charm, of children's "invented spelling", and his main point was that their spelling mistakes were quite systematic. Again and again young children, who know the letter-sound rules but who can barely read, go wrong only in that they use these rules in too literal a sense. Here are some more examples, all of them culled from the first chapter of Read's exciting book *Children's Creative Spelling* (1986).

49

Dot mak noys
My Dadaay wrx hir
This si wer mi dadaa wrx
B cwyit

How r you wan you gad i chans
sand is ol i ladr
(How are you? When you get a chance send us all a letter)

Fas (Face)
Da (day)
Kok (coke)
Lafft (left)
Likt (liked)
Watid (waited)
Wotid (wanted)

Most of the children who were studied by Read knew the names of the alphabetic letters as well as of their sounds, and that led to one of the most persistent confusions. They often represented the sound in a word by a letter name rather than by the letters' sounds. We have already had the example of "cr". There are many others in Read's data: such as "lade" for "lady", "u" for "you", and "junur" for "junior". But, although these are mistakes, they plainly show that these children used letters to represent sounds.

Read makes this point but takes it further in a most surprising way. He also claims that young children's invented spellings reveal that the children often perceive and use phonological properties that adults no longer distinguish. Furthermore (and this is the most provocative part of Read's argument), the reason that adults fail to grasp the phonological distinctions which young children make quite regularly is that the adults' knowledge of spelling actually prevents them from doing so. Children's spelling mistakes show that they are aware of phonetic distinctions which the adult has lost as a direct result of learning to spell properly.

One of the most consistent examples of this is Read's discovery that children frequently write "chr-" at the beginning of words or syllables which start with a "tr-" in conventional spelling. He found that they would write "chribls" for "troubles", "chrac" for "truck", and "aschray" for "ashtray". The significance of this, as Read points out, is that the children are right to do so. It is, in a way, misleading to represent the sound signified by "t-" in truck with the letter "T", because this sound is actually more like the "ch" sound chosen by the young children. There is a perfectly good phonetic account of this, as Read explains when he writes: "the /t/ of "trip" is not the same as the /t/ of "tip". It is affricated ... like the sound in "chip", which is essentially /t/ plus /s/ (sh)" (p. 20). It seems that young children can represent a phonetic distinction which most adults have long since ceased to notice because they know so much about spelling.

Read's research on its own is enough to convince us that children attend to, depend on and use (often with startling ingenuity), the relations between letters and sounds in order to spell words. As Read says, "they already recognise a system of phonetic properties and relations, and in terms of it, they create abstract spellings" (p. 341).

Whatever the phonological unit that young children use when they spell, it is quite plain that they do spell phonologically. Both Read (1986) and Treiman (1985a) have shown in simple experiments that the "mistakes" that children make in their invented spelling really do represent their awareness of sounds. Read showed some six year old children several pictures and asked them to choose the ones whose names began with the same sound as "truck". The names either began with "tr" ("train"), or with "t" ("turkey") or with "ch" ("chair"). He also showed them some other pictures and asked which began like "dragon". In this case the names of the pictures began with "dr", "d", or "j". In both cases about 30% of the children judged that the "ch" words began like "truck" and the "j" words like "dragon". It seems quite likely that these are the children who would spell "truck" with a "ch" and "dragon" with a "j".

Treiman went one step further than this. She read out some nonsense words to a group of five year old children and asked them to say which ones began with a "t" or a "d" sound. The children made different mistakes. Some judged that nonsense words like "tra" and "dru" did not begin with, respectively, a "t" or with a "d". These same children tended to be the ones who spelled words like "tra" and "dru" with, in the first case, a "ch" and in the second a "j". There is a definite connection between the way that these children analyse sounds and their spelling.

Speech Units in Invented Spelling

It is quite clear that children's invented spellings reflect their own awareness of sounds, which in some ways is different from and rather better than an adult's. But as we have seen there are different levels of phonological awareness, and one of the most important distinctions that has been made is between awareness of phonemes and of the intra-syllabic units, onset and rime.

Children's invented spelling suggests that they write words at both levels. The spelling definitely shows that the children attend to phonemes and try to represent them with letters, but it also demonstrates that the onset-rime division continues to have a big effect. A child who writes a word like "sowemeg" for "swimming" is plainly translating some, though not all, of the phonemes into letters. That child represents the onset, the two-phoneme sound "sw", with more than one letter: in fact she actually adds a quite plausible phoneme in her representation of the onset. If she had produced the conventional spelling "sw-" we could have wondered whether she had learned in a rote way that this is how to represent that particular onset even though she does not understand what the two letters stand for. Her unconventional rendering of this onset is proof that she understands that the onset can be broken down into phonemes.

So onset and rime seem to play a part as well in this spelling. Rebecca Treiman (1983) collected all of the spelling errors made by first grade children in Indiana. These children also relied on a phonological strategy for their earliest spelling attempts, and made many of the same phonetic distinctions discovered by Read, such as "chrap" for "trap". They too used the sounds of letter names to spell words, producing spellings like "bab" for "baby".

Treiman also noted that sometimes invented spelling does not consist entirely of translations of phonemes into letters. The children often seemed to be using a single letter to represent the intra-syllabic units onset and rime. For example, children have difficulty in analysing the onset "bl" for the word "blow" into "b" and "l", and so invent a spelling for the entire "bl" cluster (usually "b").

In Treiman's sample of children's invented spelling it turned out that the children left out a consonant if it was part of a consonant cluster, and particularly if it was the second or third sound in such a cluster, more often than if it was a single consonant. "Hasak" instead of "haystack" and "set" instead of "street" are good examples. So they often write the onset as one letter and this may mean that they think that letters represent intra-syllabic units rather than phonemes. What about rime? Treiman argues that the unusual way in which children use the names rather than the sounds of letters often shows that they are trying to represent a whole rime by a single letter. "Cr" for "car" was our example: "Bl" for "bell" is one of hers.

Treiman's explanation for these mistakes is cogent, but it is not the only one. The children may have had difficulties with clusters simply because clusters are difficult and not because they constitute the onset. They may use the names of letters to represent rimes because of a genuine confusion between letter names and letter sounds: as it happens many letter names take a VC form (F,L,M,R) and therefore are likely to coincide with rimes which also begin with a vowel and usually end with a consonant.

We need further evidence on the phonological units which children use when they spell, and Treiman herself together with Bruck (Bruck and Treiman, unpublished) have tried to provide this. They gave a group of six and seven year old children some words to spell, and they also put these children through a task rather similar to the task of Treiman's that we described in the previous chapter. The children had to recognise whether a consonant such as "s" or "l" was present in some words which were spoken to them: this target sound was either a phoneme on its own (e.g. "saip" and "aloi") or it was part of a cluster ("spoi" and "glau"). In the spelling task some of the words which children had to write contained consonant clusters ("blow, "free"), and the others single consonants ("peel", "leaf").

Once again the children found it harder to recognise the presence of a consonant when it was part of a cluster than when it was on its own. But that was not all. The second consonant in the cluster was harder to spot than the first. This was particularly interesting because, as we have already seen, children tend to keep the first consonant and leave out the second one when they spell only part of a cluster. This looks like a direct connection between a specific way of detecting sounds and an equally specific spelling pattern.

The fact that the same children did both tasks meant that Bruck and Treiman could find out whether the same children made both kinds of mistake. There was a definite relation. This is strong evidence that children do spell in a phonological manner. The way that they spell is determined by the nature of their phonological awareness.

However, this interesting result does not establish that the children make these mistakes because they find it difficult in both tasks to break up the onset. Once again it is impossible to distinguish between breaking up a cluster and breaking up a speech unit. These children may be trying to spell onsets and rimes with single letters, but we cannot be certain. Nevertheless, we have now seen a great deal of evidence for a strong connection between children's awareness of sounds and the way that they spell.

CONVENTIONAL SPELLING AND THE PHONOLOGICAL CODE

Perhaps we should temper our enthusiasm for children's invented spelling with some caution. Charming and ingenious as written words like "chrak" and "noys" may be, they are not, if one can use the phrase, real spelling. These written words are mistakes in terms of conventional spelling. Children's invented spelling is often wrong because the children seem to be using a phonological code too literally when they spell. This of course is not really a surprise, because it is impossible to spell English properly just on the basis of letter-sound relationships. No one who relies just on a phonological code will ever spell "laugh", "ache" or even "have" properly.

In fact it would be wrong to claim that young children only rely on letter-sound relationships when they start to learn to spell. There are signs that from the beginning they understand that there is more to spelling than a rigid translation of sounds into letters. To take one example, even beginning spellers manage on the whole to put the letter "s" and not the letter "z" at the end of plural words like "bells" or "ways", even though "z" is a better way of representing the actual sound at the end of these words. So from the start they seem to have an idea of at least one orthographic rule: that most plurals end in "s".

But as they get older they clearly learn more and more about spelling patterns. They begin to adopt conventional spelling and to be able to get the spelling of words right even when this spelling bears very little relation to the usual letter-sound relationships. So we have to ask ourselves whether the early stage of invented spelling has any connection with what happens later when children learn conventional spelling.

There are two possible answers to this question. One is that there is no connection: that children begin to spell in an entirely phonological manner that is hopelessly inappropriate to English spelling, and later abandon this strategy in place of a new one which does cope with the vagaries of the English orthography. This would have to be a non-phonological code and presumably either a visual or an orthographic one. The second possibility is that the stage of invented spelling is one of the first steps, that children continue to rely quite heavily on a phonological code when spelling, and that, as they become more experienced, they add other codes as well. With experience they begin to use orthographic knowledge and visual memory as well.

Thus our question is whether children use a phonological code for a while and then abandon it later on, or whether they continue to rely on this code but supplement it with other ways of spelling as they become more experienced. Is there continuity as children change from invented to conventional spelling, or is there a complete change?

A Visual Basis for Spelling

If children were to change strategies, the change would have to be to a non-phonological code. One possibility, of course, is that they might at some stage adopt a global strategy for spelling. They might spell by remembering the word as a whole—either as a pattern or as a prolonged spelling sequence—and then write by reproducing the pattern or sequence.

There have been suggestions that children do spell in this way. Most people who have put this idea forward have concentrated on the idea that children use their visual memory in order to spell. What exactly does the idea mean? There must be more to it than just remembering the word's outline—the so-called "word envelope". That might help us to read, but surely not to spell. When we write words we have to produce the individual letters. So if we rely on visual memory, that memory must be for sequences of letters.

The first convincing evidence that visual memory might play a part in spelling came from an unusual source. A long time ago Gates and Chase (1926) suggested that deaf people are at an advantage over the rest of us when it comes to spelling. We tend, Gates and Chase argued, to be stumped by the unpredictability of the English orthography and we easily forget how words like "laugh" or "choir" should be spelled because the letters do not correspond very well to the sounds in the words. Gates and Chase thought that deaf people do not rely on the letter-sound relationships nearly so much because, being deaf, they are not so aware of the sounds anyway. Gates and Chase went on to make two further claims: one was that deaf people tend to rely on visual memory when spelling more than hearing people do: the second was that as a consequence the unpredictability of English spelling should not worry them so much. Deaf people therefore should actually spell words more accurately than others do.

They tested this idea by comparing a group of deaf children with some children whose hearing was normal. The children in the two groups had reached roughly the same stage in reading. Nevertheless, the deaf children did much better than the hearing group in a test of spelling. This is an extraordinary result: a perceptually handicapped group actually surpassed a comparable normal group in spelling. Gates and Chase's explanation—that the deaf children do so well because they are better than other children at spelling words that do not conform to phonological rules—seems convincing, but we need more data to be sure that it is right. If it is right the deaf children should be better only at spelling words which cannot be constructed phonologically.

Many years later Barbara Dodd (1980) provided this extra evidence. She repeated the Gates and Chase study, but added an important refinement. The words that she gave the deaf and hearing children to spell fell into two categories: regular words like "punish", in which the letters represented the words' sounds, and irregular ones like "receipt", where the correspondence between letters and sounds was not so close. She argued that if Gates and Chase's idea was right the deaf children should only be at an advantage with the irregular words which cannot be written on the basis of letter-sound relationships.

Her comparison was between some deaf children who were 14 years old and a group of 14 year olds whose hearing was normal. In fact the two groups of children spelled as well as each other, but the deaf children were worse at spelling regular words and better with the irregular words than the other children. To put the results of this interesting study another way, the hearing children made far fewer errors with the regular than with the irregular words, while the deaf children made as many errors with one kind of word as with the other.

Thus the interesting idea developed by Gates and Chase so long ago has turned out to be an extremely fruitful one. Dodd's study makes it clear that deaf children are much less susceptible than the rest of us to irregularities in the relations between letters and sounds. Deaf people rely more on other strategies. These are plainly not phonological, but are they, as Gates and Chase suggested, necessarily visual? It does not follow. Deaf children may rely on remembering spelling sequences, in the form either of orthographic rules or of particular spelling sequences in particular words. This sort of orthographic memory need not be visual. The child might simply remember the sequence of letters in the word "receipt" without having a notion of the visual appearance of the word as a whole. So, there is a need for a test which distinguishes children's visual memory of the whole word, and their memory (which could be quite non-visual) for the sequence of letters in the words.

Some time ago, Farnham-Diggory and Simon (1975) set out to devise such a task. These two experimenters thought that the typical child learns spelling patterns visually, and they realised a need to distinguish between visual and orthographic factors in spelling. The aim of their study, which we are about to describe, was to make that distinction.

If visual memory is important in spelling, they argued, then a child who has just looked at a written word will as a result be in a better position to spell it later because she will have a fresh and strong visual image of what the word looks like. But if you show a child a written word you are also giving her information about the sequence of the word's letters—its orthography. You need another condition in which the child is given information about the sequence of letters but not about the word's visual appearance. Therefore, Farnham-Diggory and Simon designed a three-stage experiment to test this idea.

In the first stage of the experiment there were two conditions. The children, who were eight years old, were either shown ten written words quite briefly (the visual presentation) or they heard each of these words being spelled out letter by letter (the auditory presentation). The words were either meaningful ("apple", "October", "dream") or nonsense words ("plape", "amdre", "merfar"). The second stage was a brief interpolated task which lasted 15 seconds. In the third stage (the spelling task) the children had to spell the 10 words, and the question of course was whether they would do so better with the help of the visual than of the auditory presentation. Farnham-Diggory and Simon expected the visual presentation to be more effective because it gave the child a chance to see the pattern of each word.

The children did spell the words more accurately after the visual presentation than after hearing the words spelled out letter by letter, as the experimenters expected. Farnham-Diggory and Simon concluded that children depend on visual memory to a large extent in order to spell.

But this conclusion may not be the right one. The problem is that the difference between the two conditions may have had nothing to do with the fact that one presentation was visual and the other not. There was another striking difference between the visual and auditory presentations, as Henderson and Chard (1980) point out. In the "visual" presentation each word was presented as a whole, all at once. In the auditory presentation, on the other hand, the letters were presented one by one successively. One result of this difference is that the children may have been able to recognise and decipher the words much more easily in the visual than in the auditory condition.

This could have had an effect on their spelling. It is quite a reasonable suggestion that they might have been helped more when they could decipher the words in the first stage of the study than when they could not. Thus the visual presentation could have led to better spelling simply because the children could work out what the words actually were more successfully in the visual than in the auditory presentation.

The only way to sort this out is to check how well the children could decipher the words during the visual and auditory presentations, and also to work out what connection there is between being able to read the word in the first part of the experiment and being helped to spell it later on. Farnham-Diggory and Simon's data are not complete and we cannot accept their conclusion that children base their knowledge of spelling on visual memory. As we shall see, other studies demonstrate that phonological strategies continue to play a crucial role in children's spelling right through their school years. One should not dismiss the visual strategy as unimportant, but there do not seem to be any reasons at the moment for accepting it as the chief factor in children's spelling.

Regularity, Irregularity and Ambiguity

In spelling, as in reading, there are regular words, exception words and ambiguous words. We can use as examples the three simple words "dish", "said" and "beef".

"Dish" is a regular word from the point of view of spelling, and by that we mean that practically all the words that rhyme with "dish" are spelled in the same way. "Said" is an exception word: most words that rhyme with "said" end with the letters "-ed". So if children rely on letter-sound relations when they spell, they would want to spell "said" as "sed".

"Beef" is an example of an ambiguous word, as far as spelling is concerned. There are several ways to spell the long "e" sound. The double "e" is one, but we also have "ie" ("chief") and "ea" ("leaf"). So someone who wants to spell "beef" and is relying on letter-sound relationships to do so has at least three options. She has no sure way of working out which of these three is the right one if she relies just on a phonological code. There is an interesting asymmetry here. Words that are ambiguous from the point of view of spelling can be quite regular as far as reading is concerned. "Beef" is an example. Words that end in "-eef" invariably rhyme with "beef", because double "e's" always signify the same sound. On the other hand, exception words like "said" tend to be exceptions both in spelling and in reading.

So if children use a phonological code to spell it should be harder for them to spell exception and ambiguous words than entirely regular ones. Of course, these irregularities and ambiguities would only be a nuisance to them if they do concentrate on the word's sounds. A child using a visual code would cope as well with the words "said" and "beef" as with "dish", because she would treat each word in the same way as a distinctive visual pattern.

There is now considerable evidence that exception and ambiguous words are hard to spell. Doctor, Antoine and Scholnick (1989), for example, found that children between the ages of eight and 12 years made more mistakes when writing ambiguous words than when they spelled words with unambiguous spelling patterns.

Waters, Bruck and Seidenberg (1985) gave a group of eight year old children regular, exception and ambiguous words to spell and to read. The exception words were a great deal harder to spell and to read than the regular words were. Here is evidence that children of eight years do rely on a phonological code when they read and when they spell. But there was a different pattern with the ambiguous words. They were no harder than the regular words in the reading task, but the children (who could spell reasonably well) made more mistakes when they tried to write these words than they did with regular ones. These children often spelled sounds in ambiguous words in a way that would have been right in another word (e.g. "beaf" for "beef").

This is further evidence for a strong connection between children's awareness of sounds and their spelling. They link sounds with letters and with sequences of letters ("ee" "ea"), and they use these connections in their writing. Notice that we are dealing now with children who are well beyond the stage of invented spelling. Yet the relationship between letters and sounds still plays a significant part in the way that they spell. Their reliance on phonological awareness when they first begin to write words is no flash in the pan.

DO CHILDREN READ AND SPELL IN DIFFERENT WAYS?

The data that we have just looked at on young children's spelling make a striking contrast with experimental studies of the way that they read. It is, as we have seen, extremely difficult to find any convincing sign that children do read in a phonological way. No such difficulty faces us when we turn to spelling. What is the reason for this difference? One possibility is that at first children read and spell words in quite different ways.

Some words lend themselves to a phonological code more than others do (the word "cat" should be a better bet than the word "one" for anyone relying on grapheme-phoneme correspondences), and some words no doubt are easier than others to recognise as familiar patterns. There seems no reason why there should be any connection between the words which suit a phonological code and those that are more appropriate for a visual code.

This gives us a good way to look at the idea that children read words in one way and write them in quite a different way. In that case there should be little correspondence between the words which they find easy to read and those which they manage to spell without any difficulty. What, in practice, would this mean?

Suppose that we collect a list of words and ask some children to spell these words on one occasion and to read them on another. We would know then whether they could read each of these words and whether they could spell them, and that would allow us to see what the correspondence is between the words that they can read and the ones that they can spell properly.

If we think about an individual child and we categorise each of the words in the list on the basis of whether she reads and spells them, it is easy to see that each word would fall into one of four possible categories:

1. If the list is not too difficult there would, no doubt, be some words which she managed to read and also to spell correctly (*R and S words*)
2. The list could, and probably would, contain some words which she could neither read nor spell (*neither R nor S words*)
3. It is also possible that there would be words which she could read, and yet did not manage to spell (*R not S words*)
4. In principle, it is possible that the child would be able to spell some of the words correctly, without being able also to read these particular words (*S not R words*).

It is easy to see that three of these categories are normal occurrences which fit in with common sense views of children's reading and writing. On the other hand, the fourth would be a definite surprise.

One expects children to be able to read some familiar words and to spell them as well (*R and S words*) even at the earliest stage of learning about written language. One would also expect that they would be defeated on both counts (*neither R nor S words*) by some of the more difficult and less familiar words. Nor would it be a surprise if they could read some words which they were unable to spell (*R not S words*): adults, after all, have the same experience. We are used to being able to recognise written words like "diarrhoea" but then forgetting how to spell them correctly, and we readily attribute this discrepancy to the fact that it is easier on the whole to recognise spoken and written words than to recall and produce them.

But suppose that we were to find the other kind of discrepancy as well: suppose that occasionally children manage to spell particular words properly and yet fail to read them on another occasion (*S not R words*). That would be surprising to an adult: on the whole we can be fairly sure that we will be able to recognise any word that we can also spell properly. What then would we conclude if we were to find this surprising pattern in children?

Before we try to answer the question, let us see first whether it needs to be answered. In two studies, Bradley and Bryant (1979) and Bryant and Bradley (1980) gave six and seven year old children lists of words to read and to write on different occasions. They found evidence for all four categories. There were words which particular children could both read and spell, and words which they failed either to read or spell properly. A lot of the children could read some words and yet were unable to spell them—an expected discrepancy: but there were also a lot of instances of the opposite discrepancy. Many of the children could spell some words and yet failed to read them.

A plausible explanation for this two-way discrepancy (some words read but not spelled, others spelled but not read) is that there is some independence between the two activities. The children probably read and spell in different ways to some extent. However, there is another possible explanation, which is that there is a certain capriciousness in children's reading and spelling. They may read and spell words correctly on some occasions but not on others. So when, for example, a child spells a word correctly but does not manage to read it, this may be a word that she often does read but happens not to on this particular occasion.

There are two reasons for thinking that the first, and not the second, explanation is the right one. First, there was a clear and consistent difference in the type of words which children read but did not spell and those which they spelled but did not read. The commonest *R not S words* were: "light", "school", "train", and "egg", and it can be seen at a glance that these do not lend themselves well to a grapheme-phoneme correspondence strategy. The sounds associated with the letters simply do not add up to the sounds of the words. In contrast, the most frequent *S not R words* were "bun", "mat", "leg", and "pat", and these are all just right for a phonological code. The clear difference in the two types of word suggests that children use letter-sound relations in order to spell (and thus write words like "bun" correctly) but not in order to read. For reading they rely on their ability to recognise familiar words as wholes (although not necessarily as visual wholes), which allows them to read words like "school" but not to spell them.

Some results from a further experiment provide the second reason for thinking that young children's reading and spelling are independent. According to this idea they should begin to read the words which they normally can spell but not read, if they are encouraged to read phonologically. The reasoning behind this prediction is that the child's phonological code will be adequate for *S not R words* since she can spell them, but not for her *neither R nor S words* because they are words that she cannot spell.

One way to make children adopt a phonological code when they are reading is to give them nonsense words to read. These by definition are unfamiliar, and so the only way for children to decipher them is phonologically. In their second experiment Bryant and Bradley (1980) gave each child a list of nonsense words to read, and they also embedded in this list all the words that previously the particular child had not been able to read. This meant that the list of nonsense words also contained all the *S not R words* and all the *neither R nor S words* for that child. (Note that this means that different children would have been given different words.) The prediction was that the presence of the nonsense words would help the child read her *S not R words* but not her *neither R nor S words*.

The prediction was successful. Children began to read their *S not R words* much more than their *neither R nor S words* in the embedded list. Yet there was no such difference, and much less improvement, in a control condition when the children had to read both sets of words, this time embedded among other meaningful words. The study demonstrates a striking difference in the way that children read and spell.

This difference is probably a great deal stronger among beginning readers than among older children. Bryant and Bradley found virtually no *S not R words* in children older than seven years.

Concurrent Vocalisation

If children rely mainly on the phonological code in order to spell and on a visual or an orthographic strategy when they read, concurrent vocalisation ought to have a completely different effect on spelling than it does on reading. In the previous chapter we showed that children seem to be able to read words at the same time as repeating a word or sound over and over again without much difficulty. According to the argument that we have just been developing, spelling ought, in complete contrast, to be particularly vulnerable to concurrent vocalisation. This is exactly what Bryant and Bradley (1983) found. They gave six and seven year old children a set of pictures and asked them to write the name of each picture beside it. Sometimes the children wrote the words in silence, and at other times they had to repeat the incantation "bla, bla" all the while.

This time the requirement to say "bla, bla" had a serious effect: the children made many more spelling mistakes in that condition than when they had to write in silence. So concurrent vocalisation impairs children's (or at any rate English children's) spelling but not their reading, and this result supports the idea that children rely on the phonological code much more when they spell than when they read.

One has to be a little cautious, however, about this conclusion. It is just possible that the reason that the children were so held back by concurrent vocalisation is something to do with writing. Perhaps children cannot write and do something else at the same time. To check this we have to look once again at Japanese children. If concurrent vocalisation holds up spelling because it gets in the way of the act of writing in general, then it will have the same dampening effect on writing kanji as it does on writing kana. But if, as our hypothesis goes, it puts a brake on spelling because it gets in the way of the phonological code, Japanese children should be able to write kanji with ease and kana only with great difficulty if at the same time they have to repeat a sound incessantly.

Kimura and Bryant (1983; in the study that we mentioned in Chapter 2) also looked at spelling. First they confirmed Bryant and Bradley's (1983) demonstration that concurrent vocalisation makes it much more difficult for seven year old English children to spell words properly. Then they gave Japanese seven year olds two spelling/writing tasks (again they had to write the correct words beside a set of pictures): in one the children had to write kana and in the other kanji words. It was much harder for the children to write kana words when they had to say a word repeatedly at the same time than when they were writing silently: with kanji words on the other hand there was no such difference between the two conditions. So concurrent vocalisation gets in the way of children when they are trying to write a phonological script, but not when they are writing logograms. Thus concurrent vocalisation does not always hamper children's attempts to write words. It seems quite reasonable to conclude that it impairs English children's attempts to spell words because it disrupts the phonological code. It follows too that concurrent vocalisation leaves children's reading unscathed because they do not rely on the phonological code nearly as much when they read. Once again we can conclude that (1) there is a strong connection between phonological awareness and children's spelling; and (2) that it is extremely hard to find any sign of a similar connection when we look at children's reading.

CONCLUSIONS

The contrast between the work on children's reading and on their spelling strikes us as being quite remarkable. It was difficult for us to find any direct and convincing evidence that children use phonological awareness in order to read in the work that we reviewed in the previous chapter on reading. But in this chapter we find abundant evidence that children depend on a phonological code when they are working out how to spell words. Evidently, they set about reading and spelling in different ways, and there is another difference too. We can find no sign at all of a global strategy, or of a logographic stage, in children's spelling, despite Farnham-Diggory and Simon's (1975) brave attempts to demonstrate one. The contrast between children's reading and spelling seems extremely sharp to us.

The clear evidence that children use letter-sound relationships in order to spell brings us back to the distinction which we discussed in the first two chapters—the distinction between awareness of phonemes and awareness of onset and rime. There was some evidence from the data on invented spelling that children can break up onsets into phonemes when they spell. But we still do not know whether onset and rime play a part in their spelling. The next chapter, which deals with the inferences that children make about sequences of letters and their relation to onsets and rimes, will show that these speech units do play a part in children's spelling as well as in their reading.

CHAPTER 4

How Children Read and Write New Words

PHONOLOGICAL SCRIPTS AND
UNFAMILIAR WORDS

One of the great advantages of any script which represents sounds is that it allows us to cope with written words that we have never seen before. We may not always be right when we try to decipher a new word, particularly when it is written in as irregular a script as English, but we can always make a reasonable attempt to do so.

Unfamiliar words written in a logographic script are more of a problem. Each new word is a new pattern. Japanese children, for example, are able to read any new word put before them if it is written in kana, the script in which symbols represent syllables, after only two years or so of learning this extremely regular script. However, they continue to learn kanji words right through their school days.

How exactly do we work out what an entirely unfamiliar word, written in an alphabetic script, means? A global or logographic code, as we have just seen, is no use at all. What about a phonological code? In principle, it ought to do the trick. When a child sees the word "nip" for the first time she will probably know what sounds the letters "n", "i", and "p" signify, and she could, in principle, put these sounds together to work out what the word means. The trouble is that there is precious little evidence (see Chapter 2) that children who are learning to read adopt this strategy, and quite a lot of evidence that they find it very hard to do so.

Does that mean that the English child learns to read words in the same way as a Japanese child learns new kanji words? This seems unlikely because it takes the Japanese child much longer to master the kanji symbols. One has to look for another way in which English children manage to take advantage of the alphabetic system. The solution, it seems to us, is that children may adopt a quite different way to work out how to pronounce unfamiliar written words. They may do so by drawing analogies between familiar and unfamiliar written words, and using these analogies to work out pronunciations for the new words.

Suppose that a child can read "light" but has never seen the written word "fight" before. She could in principle make a direct inference from one word to the other. She could recognise that the new word ends with the same four letters as the familiar one, and could then infer that the two words end with the same sound too. The only extra thing that she needs to know in order to decipher the word as "fight" is the sound that usually goes with the letter "f". Thus, knowing how to pronounce the written word "light" can help her to read the word "fight", and knowing the word "beak" should help her to read the word "weak".

Notice that the familiar and unfamiliar words in these examples are rhyming words. The ease with which young children rhyme and detect rhyme and alliteration is a good reason for treating the idea that children read new words by making analogies seriously. When children rhyme they are in effect putting words into categories: these are categories of words with the same end sounds. When children play with alliteration they are also forming categories, this time by the beginning sounds. So children who are beginning to learn to read will already know that words like "light", "fight" and "night" have a sound in common (their rime), and this should make it easier for them to realise that these words may share a common spelling pattern as well. A young child who is skilled at recognising rhyme, and who has already put words into rhyming categories before she begins school, may quickly discover that words which sound the same are generally spelled the same.

So far we have only talked about the similarity between categorising words by rhyme (or by alliteration) and categorising them by their spelling patterns. But this connection is directly relevant to the question of analogies too. For, once a child has recognised the connection between the two categories, she is in a position to use rhyme to make inferences about unfamiliar written words. She should be able to infer that a new word which shares a spelling pattern with a word that she does know and can read also shares a sound with that familiar word. Once she realises what that sound is, she can make the inference about the new word.

This idea has little to do with single letter-sound relationships. The spelling patterns shared by words which rhyme tend to be sequences of several letters. For example, "-ight" is the sequence which "fight" and "light" share; "-eak" connects "beak" and "peak", and so on. So if children do make analogies that are based on their obvious capacity to recognise rhyme and alliteration, these analogies must involve strings of letters. This notion might seem quite implausible at first: on the face of it one letter seems easier to learn about than two or three. However, we shall show that children do recognise and use orthographic sequences at a very early stage of reading and spelling.

Another point about the idea that children make analogies in order to read new words is that it raises once again the question of the speech unit which children use. If, as we have suggested, children base these inferences on rhyme and alliteration—if they infer that two words which start or end with the same spelling pattern also start or end with the same sound as each other—then it is quite likely that these inferences work through onset and rime. Children may make connections mainly between words which have the same onset or the same rime.

ANALOGIES AND READING

Analogies with Exception Words

Several people have recognised how important analogies may be to children who are learning how to read. The most outstanding initial work on the topic was done by George Marsh and his colleagues. It was they who pointed out how great a help analogies might be to a child who is learning to read, and they also were the first to make a distinction between the use of grapheme-phoneme rules on the one hand and an analogy about an orthographic sequence on the other. An analogy, they argued, is about sequences of letters, and even makes it possible for us to read new words which could not be read on a simple letter-by-letter basis ("light"-"fight").

So these experimenters decided to look at the way in which children manage to read entirely unfamiliar words. These words were nonsense words, because Marsh and his colleagues wanted to make sure that the children had not seen them before. Each of the nonsense words had a spelling pattern in common with a particular real word, and the experimenters were careful to make sure that the analogous real word was one which could not be read on the basis of simple grapheme-phoneme rules.

Marsh and his colleagues called their method the "conflict" technique. The "conflict" was between spelling by analogy and using grapheme-phoneme rules. We can see how this worked by taking an example of one of their nonsense words—"puscle". This is spelled in the same way as the real word "muscle". Marsh and colleagues argued that children would read "puscle" as though it rhymed with "muscle" if they were making an analogy. However, if they were using grapheme-phoneme rules, they should produce a word sounding like "puskle".

They asked children aged 10 and 16 years and also college students either to read aloud a list of 10 nonsense words of this type, or to choose a pronunciation for the same nonsense words from two possible pronunciations provided by the experimenter (Marsh, Desberg & Cooper, 1977). One of these was the "analogous" pronunciation, and the other the word that one would pronounce after using grapheme-phoneme rules.

In both tasks Marsh and his colleagues found that the younger readers made fewer analogies than the older children or the students did. The ten year olds used grapheme-phoneme rules more often than analogies. The older children and the students in contrast took advantage of analogies more frequently than they used the grapheme-phoneme rules.

Marsh, Friedman, Welch and Desberg (1980a) used the same conflict technique in another experiment, but this time the words that they were interested in, instead of being presented on their own, were embedded in prose passages. They gave these to children aged seven and ten years and also to college students. Each passage included some nonsense words and it was clear from the rest of the sentence that these words stood for nouns. Some of the nonsense words were there to assess the child's use of analogy in the same way as in the study that we have just described (e.g. "faugh" would be pronounced "faf" by analogy to "laugh" (Californian English), but "faw" via spelling-sound rules).

Marsh and his colleagues reported that the seven year old children made very few analogies: they made them, on average, with only 14% of the words. The 10 year olds and the college students made analogies more often (34% and 38% of the time respectively). So in this study the main change was between 7 and 10 years, and this time there was not much difference between 10 year old children and college students. Can we conclude from this that young children make few analogies about new words, and that this kind of inference is really only important at the later stages of learning to read?

We think that this would be too pessimistic. There are two reasons, in our view, why the studies by Marsh and his colleagues may paint too bleak a picture of the readiness of young children to make inferences about new words. One is that these children may not have known the analogous words as well as the older children did. You can only make analogies about words like "puscle", "tepherd" and "biety" if you can read and can remember the spelling patterns of the analogous words "muscle", "shepherd" and "piety". It is quite possible that the younger children simply did not know the analogous written words, or at any rate did not know them well enough to use them as a basis for analogies.

The other difficulty is the use that Marsh and his colleagues made of nonsense words. They had a good reason for giving the children such words, as we have seen, but nevertheless the words could have had an effect on the results. In Chapter 3 we saw that there is evidence from the study by Bryant and Bradley (1980) that children are more likely to turn to grapheme-phoneme rules when they read nonsense words than when they are given real words. So the nonsense words that Marsh and his colleagues used could have encouraged the children to read them letter by letter and could thus have deterred them from making as many analogies as they would have done when reading normal words.

In fact another study by the same group (Marsh, Friedman, Desberg & Saterdahl, 1981) shows that young children can draw analogies about new words provided that they realise that such analogies are possible. In this study the experimenters again asked the children—seven and nine year old children—to read a list of nonsense words. But this time they also gave the children a list of the real word analogues, and told them that the nonsense words had been made by changing one letter of the real words. The seven year old children made analogies 78% of the time and the nine year olds 92% of the time. So young children do well if they are told that they can make an analogy and how it is to be made.

What is one to make of this last result? It certainly shows that young children are perfectly capable of making analogies (even about nonsense words) if they are told how to do so. But, though this is useful information for teachers, it does not mean that young children do actually make inferences about analogous words in a spontaneous way when reading. Nevertheless, the considerable success of the younger children in this remarkable study is an encouragement to look further for evidence that analogies play a part in children's reading.

Analogies in Transfer Experiments

The results of a study that was done quite some time ago point in this direction. This was done by Baron in 1977. There were two stages to his experiment. In the first he taught kindergartners—five year olds—to read a set of simple words and also a set of sounds. In the second part he set out to see whether they could use what they had learned in the first part to help them to read new words.

The children were taught words and sounds like "b", "at", "bat", "ed", and "red" in the first part. In the second part of the experiment they were given words of two types. One set of words could be read by analogy. "Bed" and "rat" are two examples of this kind of word: "bed" ends in the same way as "red", and "rat" as "mat" (once again the experimenters are interested in an analogy based on rhyme and therefore on the spelling sequence that represents the words' rime). The children would only be able to read the other type of words, according to Baron, with the help of grapheme-phoneme rules. "Bad" and "bet" are examples of such words. They do not share spelling sequences with the original words, and therefore cannot be deciphered by analogy (Fig.4.1).

The results were very striking. There was a huge difference between the two conditions. The children were able to read around 90% of the first kind of word, the kind that could be read by analogy. Yet they only managed to read 15% of the words for which analogies (according to Baron) were not possible. Baron concluded that

Training set	Set 1	Set 2	Set 3	Set 4
	b	d	s	r
	at	ug	in	ug
	bat	bug	pin	mug
	ed	am	at	an
	red	dam	sat	ran
Test words				
1. GPC + analogy	bed	dug	sin	rug
2. Analogy	rat	bam	pat	man
3. GPC correspondence	bad	bum	pit	rag
4. GPC correspondence	bet	bag	sit	run

FIG. 4.1.   Design of the experiment by Baron (1977).

young children use analogies spontaneously and naturally even at the beginning stages of reading, and that they take to this strategy much more willingly than to using grapheme-phoneme correspondences.

By and large, Baron's study does seem to demonstrate that children take to analogies very well and very soon too, but there is one reason for caution. The children were actually given explicit instruction about the rime of the words that they were learning to read and about the spelling sequence that represented it. They were told that the letters "-at" and "-ed" represented particular sounds. So they were in a better position to use this knowledge when they were given the "analogous" words ("rat" and "bed") in the second part of the experiment because these contained those same spelling sequences. Thus we cannot be sure whether the children did so well with these words because they made a genuine analogy or, more mundanely, because they applied a rule that they had just learned about a spelling sequence which represented a particular rime.

One interesting point that should be made about Baron's study is that he appears to have made an implicit assumption which, as it happens, is shared in most other work on analogies. This is that the analogy is based on the words' rimes and on the spelling sequences that represent those rimes. Analogies are, according to Marsh and to Baron, inferences that the spelling pattern which represents the rime in one word will represent it in another word as well. So when we make an analogy we work out that the written word "puscle" represents a word that rhymes with "muscle", and "rat" represents a word that rhymes with "mat". In all these examples the connection has been through the speech unit, the rime.

This assumption may be right but, in principle, there is another possibility, which is that analogies may be made about segments of speech and spelling patterns that cut across the onset-rime division. It is just possible that children might make an analogy about the spelling pattern "ba-" having read the word "bat": this analogy would be about the onset and half of the rime. Of course such an analogy may seem unlikely, given what we know about the importance of the onset-rime division in children's phonological awareness. But the possibility should not be ruled out.

Ironically, half of the words which Baron thought that the children could read only by grapheme-phoneme rules could have been read by analogy as well, if one allows that analogies which cut across the onset-rime division are possible. These words started with the same consonant-vowel units as words that the children learned in the first part of Baron's study. For example, the word "bat" did not have a rime in common with any of the words given to the children in the first part of the study, but it does start with the same consonant and vowel and the same two letters as "bad", which was one of the original words. In fact the very low performance of the children with the words which Baron thought that they would only be able to read through grapheme-phoneme correspondences suggests that they hardly ever do make analogies which involve the onset and half of the rime. But that might have been because Baron, as we have seen, deliberately drew the children's attention to the rime and the letters which represented it in the first part of the experiment. At any rate, we should bear in mind the fact that people have tended, justifiably or not, to treat analogies as dependent on rime.

There is another study which suggests that children often do make analogies about consonant-vowel sequences i.e. about the onset and half of the rime. Pick, Unze, Brownell, Drozdal and Hopmann (1978) also looked at the possibility that children make analogies about two-letter sequences in three-letter words. They taught a group of 6 year old children to read 12 words (apparently the first that these children had ever read). These were simple consonant-vowel-consonant (CVC) words such as "bug", "rug", "rat" and "fat". Then they asked the children to read CVC nonsense words which shared either the first two letters ("bup", "rad"), the last two letters ("sug", "lat") or a combination of the same grapheme-phoneme correspondences ("bap", "sut").

Thirteen of the 17 children in the study managed to read some nonsense words correctly on the first transfer trial. Most of these children were strikingly successful with words like "bup" and "rad", which share their first two letters and thus their onset plus half of their rime ("bug"-"bup") with words that they had learned to read in the first part of the study. They were actually nearly twice as good with these nonsense words as with ones which shared a rime with the initial set of words ("bug"-"sug").

So the study seems to support Baron's idea that children make analogies as soon as they begin to read, but it also suggests that these analogies need not be based on rime. However, before we accept either of these conclusions we should consider the words that Pick and her colleagues gave the children to read. These were all simple words, and there was nothing to stop the children reading them correctly by applying grapheme-phoneme rules. The original training could simply have bolstered their understanding of these rules. The reason for the children reading the words which had an opening sequence of letters in common with the original words could simply be that they paid more attention to the letters at the beginning of the words that they were taught about. We can see that Marsh's precaution of using words that would be read in one way if the children were making analogies and in another if they were using grapheme-phoneme rules was a good one. Without it we cannot be convinced by Pick's claim about analogies.

The need for this precaution led Baron to do a further study in 1979. In this he gave nine year old children three lists of words to read. Each word had its counterpart with the same spelling pattern in the other two lists. The three lists were of regular ("cut"), exception ("put"), and nonsense ("lut") words. Baron wanted to know how the children would pronounce the nonsense words. If children make analogies, then they should read each nonsense word to rhyme with a real word which has the same spelling pattern as the nonsense word and which they also know how to read, whether this is an exception or a regular word.

This was the pattern that he found. If the children could read just one of the real words in a triad of words with the same spelling pattern, they tended to read the nonsense word in that triad as rhyming with the word that they knew. He concluded that "the use of analogies is a natural mechanism for decoding nonsense words" (p.67). His conclusion seems justified, at any rate about the children in the study, but they were quite old. If he could have shown the same pattern with far younger children we could have been more convinced that children use analogies to read new words as soon as they begin to learn to read. But, of course, that would have been inconceivable with this experimental task because younger children would not have been able to read enough of the real words.

Analogies from Clue Words

The research that we have reviewed so far shows how difficult it is to find out whether or not young children, just starting to read, are able to make analogies about new words. The difficulty is this. People make analogies about new words on the basis of words which they know and can read already. Older children can read a great number of words: young children hardly any. That is why it is relatively easy to see whether older children make analogies: and that is why it is hard to find a decent test for children who are only just beginning to learn to read and write. They can read so few words that it is difficult at the start of an experiment to be sure that there are words that they can use as a basis for an analogy.

Pick and Baron's solution was to teach children words which they could then use, with the help of analogies, to work out what some entirely new written words meant. But the fact that they resorted to training meant in the end that their claims, that beginning readers make analogies about spelling sequences, are not watertight. They used words which are easy to read on a grapheme-phoneme basis and trained the children for quite long periods of time before giving them tests of analogies. They could unwittingly have taught the children about the grapheme-phoneme rules during the original training period, and that on its own would account for the children's success in the analogical problems. The children may have solved them without actually making analogies.

There is another, simpler, way to make sure that children know a word and then to see if they can use that word to make an inference about another word. It is to show a child a word which up until then she has not been able to read, and then to tell her what it says. Then you can see if the child can use this word to read analogous words which contain the same spelling sequences. Suppose, for example, that a child cannot read any of the following words: "beak", "weak" and "leak". You can show her the word "beak" and tell her how to pronounce it, and then give her the other two words and ask her to read them. If she can make analogies, then she should be able to work out the pronunciation of "weak" and "leak". This simple technique involves no lengthy training and the experimenter does not have to use words which can be spelled by applying grapheme-phoneme rules.

The method allows one to tackle a question which is implicitly raised, but never answered, by all the studies that we have reviewed so far. This is the question of the role in analogies of onset and rime. Most experimenters, with the exception of Pick and her colleagues, have assumed implicitly (the point has not been discussed explicitly) that people make analogies about spelling sequences which represent the rime. Is this right? One can look at the question using the technique that we have just described by contrasting two kinds of analogy, one based on rime ("beak"-"weak") and the other which cuts across onset and rime and involves the onset and only half of the rime ("beak"-"bean"). If, as the research that we discussed in earlier chapters suggests, onset and rime play a significant role in analogies, children should be able to make the first kind of analogy much more readily than the second.

The technique that we have just described was first tried by Goswami (1986) in a study of children aged between five and seven years. Most of the five year old children were at the very beginning stages of reading: they could read none of the words in a standardised reading test. Her experiment took the form that we have just described. The children were first given all the words to be used in the experiment and asked to read them: this was simply a pretest and its purpose was to establish which of the words each child could read. Then the children went through a series of trials which tested their ability to use clue words as a basis for analogies about new words. In each trial the child was first shown one written "clue" word, such as "beak", and was told what it said. Then she was asked to read other words, some of which shared a spelling pattern with the clue word. Sometimes this common spelling pattern represented the words' rime ("beak"-"weak"), and at other times the words' onset and half their rime ("beak"-"bean"). These were the "analogy" words, but the children were also asked to read "control" words in this part of the experiment (Fig.4.2).

The control words were there to check that the children were making genuine analogies. Some of the control words had three letters in common with the clue word: nonetheless they did not share a spelling sequence with that word [e.g. "beak" (clue word), "bask" or "lake" (control words)]. Others were words whose spelling patterns bore no particular relation. A child who makes an analogy on the basis of being able

	Beginning sounds		End sounds	
	Clue word	Clue word	Clue word	Clue word
	beak	beak	beak	beak
	Analogous word	Control word	Analogous word	Control word
	bean	bask	peak	bank

FIG. 4.2.   The first analogy experiment (Goswami, 1986): the children were given a clue word on each trial which remained visible throughout the trial, and they were then asked to read a succession of test words (analogous and control words).

to read "beak" should be able to read "weak" as a result, but not "lake". So if the children can make analogies, they should read more "analogy" words than control words.

This, in general, was what happened. The children in all three age groups (five, six and seven year olds) read the analogy words which shared a rime and a common spelling sequence signifying that rime ("beak"-"weak") better than the control words. So even beginning readers make analogies based on rime.

However, the youngest group, the five year olds, did not make the other type of analogy: they did not do any better with words which had a spelling sequence in common with the clue word when that common sequence represented the onset and half of the rime ("beak"-"bean") than with the control words. In fact, the older children did manage to make analogies with this second kind of analogy word, but to a lesser extent than with the first kind. Thus rime is an important factor in analogies, and it looks as though children start by making analogies just about spelling sequences which represent that speech unit (and as we shall see later about the onset too), and later notice spelling patterns which cut across the onset/rime division.

Young children, then, make analogies about spelling sequences that signify rimes and they probably do so without having to be taught. Do they make analogies about onsets as well? To find this out Goswami gave some six year old children a task which was like her first study in every respect except that the two kinds of analogy words were different. One kind of analogy word shared an onset (always a consonant cluster) with the clue word. So if "trim" was the clue word, "trap" would be an analogy word. The other kind shared only part of a rime (again a consonant cluster) with the clue word. With "wink" as the clue word, "tank" would be an analogy word of this type. If children base analogies on speech units, they should do better with the first kind of analogy, as it is based on the onset, than with the second, which involves dissecting the rime (Fig.4.3).

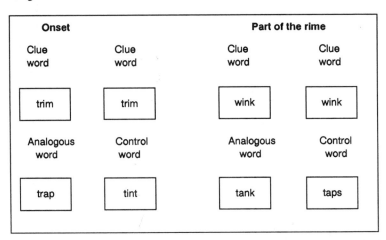

FIG. 4.3.   The analogy experiment in which analogies could be made on the basis of the "onset" of the clue word or on part of its "rime".

This was the pattern that Goswami found. The children read more of the first kind of analogy words than the second. In fact they probably did not make analogies at all with the words which shared only part of the rime with the clue words, as they read no more of these words than of the control words. In contrast they did do much better with the words that shared an onset with the clue word than with the control words. So onsets as well as rimes play a significant role in children's analogies.

The method that we have described seems a simple and straightforward test of analogies. But there is one possible objection to it. The words which five year old children could connect by analogy rhymed with each other. The experience of hearing a word might encourage a child to think of another rhyming word. So it is just possible that the children could have been "primed" by hearing the clue word to think of and produce another word which rhymed with it without even realising that the two words had the same spelling pattern. So when they say "peak" after having been shown what the written word "beak" sounds like, they may simply be coming up with a similar sound regardless of the way the analogous words are written.

We can use the irregularity of the English script to check this. One simply has to ask the children to read words which rhyme with the clue word, but which do not have the same spelling pattern, such as "head" and "said". If children are simply being "primed" to produce a rhyming word after being told how to read the word "head" (the clue word), they should be as likely to read the word "said" correctly as the word "bread". Goswami (1990a) has shown that this is not the case. In a study which was in other respects much the same as her earlier one, she found that children who are given, for example, the clue word "head" are more likely as a result to read the word "bread" than the word "said" correctly. This means that they do connect the common spelling sequence to the common rime. They are making genuine analogies about spelling patterns (Fig.4.4).

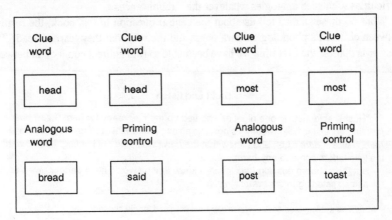

FIG. 4.4.   The material that was used in order to check that the analogies that children make while reading are not an artefact of phonological priming.

It could be said that the two experiments that we have just described are not about "real reading", because the children who took part in them only had to read single words, whereas in the real world they usually have to read connected prose. There is a lot to this objection. There is little point in being able to make analogies unless you can do so when you are reading connected passages of prose.

Goswami (1988a) has also shown that children make analogies when reading stories. The children in this study were six and seven years old. They were given a story to read with a "clue" word—a difficult one—in the title. One example is a story with the title, "Hark! and listen". "Hark" is a difficult word, and the children were told what it meant when they were given the title to read. In the following story there were other words which had spelling sequences in common with the clue word—words like "harp" and "dark", and also some control words (like the control words in the previous studies). The children were able read the analogy words in the story more often than the control words: they were also better with these analogy words than some other children who did not first learn to read the stories' titles (Fig.4.5).

The only difference between the results of this and of previous studies was that analogies about rime ("hark"-"dark") were no easier than analogies about the onset and half of the rime ("hark"-"harp"). The reason for this difference may well be that stories gave the children extra contextual cues which helped them over their usual difficulties with analogies about spelling sequences that do not represent either just an onset or just a rime.

We should like to note too that the children in this study were at least six years old and had made some headway with reading. We doubt that the context of the story would have helped five year old beginning readers to make "hark"-"harp" analogies as well. Their dependence on rime and their complete incapacity to make analogies about sequences that reflect only half a rime ("beak"-"bean") suggests that they will have difficulties with such analogies whatever the circumstances.

What do these studies tell us about the central question in this book, the relation between children's phonological awareness and the way that they learn to read? The answer is that for the first time we have been able to find a direct connection between

---

Hark! and listen

"Hush!" said mother one night as she tied up my *hair* ready for bed. "I can *hear* a *lark* singing. Listen how sweetly it sings, like an angel's *harp*." I got into bed and listened *hard*. It was a *dark* night, and I knew that the *hawk* would be out hunting. I didn't want the little lark to come to any *harm*.

But then I heard our dog *bark* loudly. I knew that he would keep danger away, so I fell asleep listening to the sweet singing.

Note. The analogy and control words were not italicised for the children.

FIG. 4.5.   Clue word analogies: story reading (Goswami, 1988a).

a phonological strategy and children's reading. Analogies are made about words which share sounds: therefore analogies are based on sounds. Thus to make an analogy is to analyse the word that one is trying to read phonologically. There seems no doubt now that children do adopt this particular type of phonological strategy as soon as they begin to learn to read.

At first they base this phonological approach on the phonological units which mean most to them—onset and rime. The data that we have on analogies fits well with what we know about children's early sensitivity to rhyme and alliteration, and as we shall see later there are empirical reasons too for making a connection between children's analogies about new words and their rhyming skills.

SPELLING

Analogies are based on phonology, and phonology plays a much stronger role in children's spelling than in their reading. So, if children make analogies about phonological units when they read unfamiliar words, there can be little doubt that they also do so when they try to spell a word for the first time. But, convincing as this suggestion is, we cannot assume that it is necessarily true. We need to look at the evidence.

In their search for analogies Marsh and his colleagues looked at children's spelling as well as at their reading (Marsh, Friedman, Welch & Desberg, 1980b; Marsh et al., 1981). They simply asked children to write nonsense words that rhymed with real words, such as "jation" which rhymes with "nation". Our spelling of this nonsense word is analogical in that we spelled it in the same way as the word that it rhymes with. But it is also possible—and there is no reason for saying this is wrong—to spell the word phonetically, in which case one would come up with something like "jayshun". Marsh and his colleagues wanted to see which strategy the children would adopt.

They worked with seven and ten year old children and with college students. They found that none of the seven year olds made any analogies at all in this spelling task. Analogies were made for 33% of the words by the ten year olds, and 50% by the college students. So the study shows that older children at least really do make analogies when they have to spell unfamiliar words.

We cannot interpret the younger children's scores with any confidence, because it is not clear whether these children could actually spell the real words on which the analogies had to be based. So there are two possible reasons for them not writing "jation": one is that they cannot use analogies to work out how to spell a new word, and the other is that they can but show no signs of doing so here because they do not know how to spell "nation" in the first place.

In fact, this group of researchers did have more success with some seven year olds in another very similar study in which they did check whether the children could spell the real words on which the spelling analogy had to be based (Marsh et al., 1981). Here the seven year olds made analogies on 26% of the nonsense words. Even seven year olds, this interesting result demonstrates, can to some extent use analogies when working out how to spell a word.

Another experimenter has also shown that children (in this case 9–12 year olds) use their knowledge of a word's spelling to work out how to write a nonsense word. Ruth Campbell (1985) used a "priming" technique in her study. She asked the children to spell nonsense words like /prein/. She told them that she would read out real and nonsense words, but that they should only write down the nonsense words. Half of the children then heard one word list, in which target nonsense words like /prein/ were preceded by real word "primes" like "crane". The other half heard a different list, in which the same target nonsense words were preceded by matching primes like "brain", words with a similar sound but with a different spelling pattern from the priming words in the other list (Fig.4.6). (A control group of children received the list of nonsense words to spell without any primes.)

The aim behind this comparison was to see whether the children would spell each nonsense word in the same way as the rhyming real word that had preceded it. Would those who heard the first list spell /prein/ as "prane", and those who heard the second list spell it as "prain"?

Only the children who were more advanced in reading (who had a reading age of 11 years or more) consistently adopted the spelling pattern in the "prime" when they wrote the nonsense words. So we can be sure that these children at any rate use similarities in sound to make analogies about spelling. However, the fact that the less advanced children did so infrequently does not necessarily mean that they do not make analogies (and indeed Campbell herself did not reach this negative conclusion). They may make analogies in the normal course of events, but not when faced with nonsense words.

Let us look, then, at an experiment which involves real words. Goswami (1988b) decided to use clue words to study analogies in spelling as well. She worked with a group of six year old children (with a spelling age of seven years). First she tested their spelling of all the words that she was to use in the experiment. The main experiment followed a few days later. In each trial in the experiment the child was shown a "clue"

Nonsense words	Prime A list	Prime B list	Primed spellings
/prein/	crane	brain	prane, prain
/fein/	crane	brain	fane, fain
/boup/	soap	rope	boap, bope
/moum/	foam	home	moam, mome
/krait/	fright	white	kright, krite
/zoul/	coal	pole	zoal, zole
/plouz/	close	toes	plose, ploes

FIG. 4.6.   Design used by Campbell (1985).

word, such as "beak", and was told what it said. This word was left on the table while the experimenter asked the child to spell some other words. Some of the words sounded similar to the clue word ("bean", "peak"), and others did not ("lake", "bask"). If children make analogies in spelling, they should be able to use "beak" as a basis for spelling "bean" and "peak", but not "lake" and "bask".

That was what Goswami found. The children spelled the analogy words better than the control words. So they seem to be able to make analogies in spelling as well as in reading, and there is another similarity between the reading studies and this experiment on spelling. The children spelled the analogy words which shared a rime with the clue word ("beak"-"weak") more often than those which shared an onset and half a rime ("beak"-"bean"). Once again analogies based on rime are easier than those that cut across onset and rime.

We find it easy to reach a conclusion about these studies. Analogies are a natural and important part of children's reading and spelling. They are made by old and young children alike—by older children who know how to read and write a great number of words and by young children who can read hardly any words and spell even fewer. These beginning readers are ready to make analogies even though they know so few written words and therefore have such a small basis for making any analogies at all. Nevertheless, they apply their awareness of rime, and their obvious capacity to make inferences, to the business of learning how to read and spell new words.

THE CONNECTION BETWEEN ANALOGY AND PHONOLOGICAL AWARENESS

It is time to bring together several themes that we have been pursuing in these first four chapters. We think that these themes can be combined into a coherent argument about children's awareness of sounds and about the use that they make of this awareness when they learn to read and write.

We began the book by showing that when children are young, and particularly during the time before they go to school, they are much more sensitive to the intra-syllabic units onset and rime than they are to single phonemes. Their alertness to these units fits well with their rhyming skills and with their interest in rhyme and alliteration generally.

Children's awareness of rhyme is especially important because it shows not just that they are aware of rimes, but also that they are able to categorise words on the basis of their sounds. These categories are of spoken words, but they could well form the basis for most of what children learn later on about spelling patterns in written words. Different words share common spelling sequences, and these are often words that have sounds in common too (e.g. "cat", "hat", "mat" or "light", "fight", "might"). If our argument is right children will be able to form categories of words which share the same onset or the same rime. They will find it easier to link words which begin with "str" or which end in "ing", than words which begin with "stri" or which end in "ng". By the same token they will learn most quickly about the spelling sequences which represent onset and rime if the spelling categories that they form are, as we suggest, based on their phonological categories.

Once children have the idea that words which have sounds in common often share spelling sequences as well, they have a powerful way to work out how to read and to spell new words. They can use the spelling pattern in one word to work out the sound of another word with the same spelling sequence, and to decide how to spell a word which rhymes with a word that they know how to spell already.

We have given you evidence for each step in this argument—for children's awareness of intra-syllabic units, for their rhyming skills, for their difficulties in recognising phonemes and thus in using grapheme-phoneme relations when they read, and finally for their use of analogies in reading and spelling. We have shown, as far as we can, that our claims for all these things are true.

But these are connected claims in a connected argument, and as far as we have gone we have dealt with each of them separately. Much of the rest of the book will deal with the connections. By reviewing work on backward readers, on correlational studies, on the effects of training and on the patterns of individual differences in learning to read, we hope to establish empirically that these connections do exist.

We will end this chapter with our first piece of evidence for a link between two parts of our argument. We have claimed that there must be a link between children's rhyming skills and the ease with which they make analogies about new words when they begin to read.

To test this idea, Goswami (1990b) looked at the relationship between children's analogies (in reading) and their performance in two different tests of phonological awareness: a test of rhyme and alliteration, and also one of phoneme deletion. Two tests were needed because the hypothesis being tested was that there is a specific link between children's analogies in reading and only one of these tests: awareness of rhyme, according to the hypothesis, is connected to analogies: phoneme awareness is not. So rhyme scores should be more closely related to the children's success in analogies in Goswami's "clue word" analogy test than phoneme awareness. And so it was. The children's scores in the rhyme test (Bradley and Bryant's oddity task) were strongly related to their success in making analogies about the beginnings ("beak"-"bean") of words and about the ends ("beak"-"weak") as well, even after controls for differences in the children's verbal ability.

In contrast their scores in the phoneme deletion test (the one devised by Content et al., 1982, and described in Chapter 1) did not predict their success in making analogies about the beginnings of words, and was much less strongly related to the children's performance in the rime analogy task than their rhyme scores were.

So there does seem to be a specific relation between children's sensitivity to rhyme and alliteration and their success in using analogies in order to read new words. We now have empirical evidence for one link between two parts of our argument. We will establish other links in the chapters that follow.

CHAPTER 5

Comparisons with Backward Readers and Spellers

When, at the end of the last chapter, we talked about the need to make connections we meant that we have to show how one skill might affect another. We have argued, for example, that children build up certain kinds of phonological sensitivities, and that these eventually help them when they begin to learn to read. But we have not shown that they do help: we have not established the connection. How does one demonstrate connections, which are really causal connections, in children's reading?

Many people have tried to do so by turning to children who have not managed to learn to read. Their difficulties ought to tell us something about the skills which children need in order to learn to read. If you can find some skill which backward readers lack but other children possess in abundance, you may have spotted an essential ingredient in learning to read. For example, if phonological skills play a part in learning to read, children who are particularly insensitive to phonological segments should find it difficult to learn to read. In that case at least some of the group of children whom we call "dyslexic" should do badly in phonological tasks.

With this rationale in mind, many psychologists have made comparisons between children who have fallen behind in reading with others who read as well as would be expected for children of their age. Most of these studies have been of groups of children. The experimenters have usually compared a group of backward readers with another group of children who have no particular problems with reading. Their aim has always been to find some task in which poor readers fare relatively badly.

There are different ways of comparing backward with normal readers. The one that has been most popular is known as *the age match* (Fig.5.1).

Here one compares a group of backward readers with a group of normal readers of the same age. The children in the two groups are usually alike in every respect as far

	Experimental group	Control group
Age	10 years	10 years
I.Q.	100	100
Reading level	7 years	10 years

FIG. 5.1.   Design used in age match studies.

as can be seen, except that one has difficulty with reading while the other does not. A typical age match would be a study which involves a group of 10 year old backward readers who have a normal I.Q. but whose reading age is only 8 years and therefore 2 years lower than expected. This group would be compared to another containing children with the same age and I.Q. but with a reading age of 10 years—the normal reading level for children of that age and I.Q. Thus the one obvious difference between the two groups is that one reads at a lower level than the other.

What can comparisons of this sort tell us about the skills that a child needs in order to learn to read? Age matches are quite useful in our view (Bryant & Goswami, 1986), but they have their limitations and one must recognise what these are. Age matches are useful because they provide a kind of minimum requirement. No theory about the reasons for reading difficulties can be right unless it is confirmed by positive results in an age match experiment. Suppose that you think that the reason for backward readers' difficulties is X, and then you compare a group of them with a group of normal readers of the same age and I.Q. If you find no sign at all that the backward readers are worse on X, your hypothesis cannot be right, or at any rate it cannot be right about the backward readers that you have studied. A positive result, which takes the form of the backward readers being worse on X, is a *sine qua non*. If you fail to find such a result, you should abandon your theory.

Age matches are most useful when they eliminate theories which do not fulfil this minimum requirement. There are some well known examples of this happening. Vellutino's (1979) work on visual memory and learning is one. He showed, in a series of very convincing experiments, that backward readers are as good as normal readers of the same age at remembering visual patterns. It is difficult to see how anyone can maintain the theory, popular at one time, that reading backwardness is primarily a difficulty in recognising visual patterns, in the face of negative evidence of this sort.

What about positive results in an age match? These, as we have seen, are a minimum requirement, but they are no more than that. If one finds a difference between backward and normal readers of the same age, one knows that one's hypothesis is viable, but that is all. If backward readers do turn out to be worse than their age mates in a test that measures X, the lack of X may be at the root of their problems but it need not be. There is an alternative, which is that the backward readers lack X because they have fallen behind in their reading. The lack of X may be the result of their reading backwardness and not its cause. This is not so far-fetched. As we saw in Chapter 1, there are persuasive reasons for thinking that the experience of learning to read does change children's intellectual skills. So children who fall behind in reading may as a result fall behind in these other skills too.

So the results of age match experiments either rule out ideas about the reasons for children's reading difficulties, or tell us that these ideas are worth considering further. Let us see what they tell us about the importance of phonological skills.

AGE MATCHES AND THE PHONOLOGICAL CODE

Comparisons between normal and backward readers of the same age have been very popular in general, but they have not been used much in work on children's phonological skills. The most significant example of a study of this type which deals with phonological awareness was done by the well known group at the Haskins laboratory (Liberman, Shankweiler, Liberman, Fowler & Fischer, 1978). They were interested in rhyme and memory. Their experiment was on the "confusion" effect, and before we describe the experiment we shall have to say what this effect is.

Some time ago Conrad (1964) established that adults who are asked to remember particular visually presented alphabetic letters tend to confuse those whose (letter) names sound alike (rhyme), such as "B", "C", "P" and "T": they do not have nearly so much trouble with letters like "V", "M" and "X", whose names do not rhyme. The fact that adults confuse letters whose names rhyme with one another must mean that adults categorise them, probably implicitly, as having a common sound. This is a phonological category.

Conrad then did a developmental version of this experiment. He gave children aged between 4 and 11 years a task with two conditions (Conrad, 1971). In one, they had to remember pictures whose names rhymed (cat, hat), and recognise them from amongst sets which included other pictures whose names also rhymed with the original pictures (bat, rat). In the other, the names of the pictures did not rhyme with each other.

Conrad found that the four year old children remembered the two types of pictures and their names equally well. However, children of five years and above made more mistakes with the pictures whose names rhymed than with those whose names sounded quite different from each other. This difference between the two conditions increased with age: it was much stronger in the older children than in the five year olds.

Conrad's experiment established a developmental change, and was not directly concerned with reading. It was Liberman et al. (1978) who realised a possible connection between Conrad's effect and children's reading. If phonological difficulties are a cause of reading problems, backward readers should show this effect less strongly than normal readers. These experimenters decided to test this idea in an experiment with eight year old children who were divided into superior, marginal, and poor readers. The children were given strings of five letters to recall either immediately or following a 15-second delay. The strings were either "confusable" (made up of rhyming consonants: B,C,D,G,P,T,V,Z), or "non-confusable" (made up of non-rhyming consonants: H,K,L,R,Q,S,W,Y).

The superior readers made more mistakes with the confusable (rhyming) list than with the non-confusable one. This group therefore produced the confusion effect. But the other two did not. For them one list was as easy to remember as the other. This seemed like good evidence for a difference in the way that children categorise letters. Good readers do so by rhyme: less proficient readers may not.

Three other studies have produced the same result (Mann, Liberman & Shankweiler, 1980; Siegel & Linder, 1984, Siegel & Ryan, 1988). However, other experimenters have found different results. People have been unable to replicate the effect. There was no difference in the strength of the confusion effect between good and poor readers in a study by Alegria et al. (1982), and several other experimenters have also found the effect to be equally strong in both groups (Hall, Ewing, Tinzmann & Wilson, 1981; Johnston, 1982; Byrne & Ledez, 1983; Bisanz, Das & Mancini, 1984; Morais et al., 1986b). When there are disagreements of this sort it is probably better to attend to the positive results (a difference between the two groups) than to the negative ones. There are so many possible extraneous reasons why a study should produce negative results that positive ones have slightly more value. So we ought to consider what the positive results produced by the Haskins group mean.

The results suggest that a causal hypothesis is viable. The hypothesis is that some children fall behind in reading because they do not categorise words by their sounds. But we can only say that the hypothesis is viable, not that it is definitely right. We cannot dismiss the alternative hypothesis that children form phonological categories as a result of learning to read, and thus that these categories are less well formed in poor readers as a direct result of their lack of progress in reading.

READING LEVEL MATCHES AND THE PHONOLOGICAL CODE

We cannot be satisfied with the conclusion that an idea is viable: we need to know whether it is right or not. Is there some other kind of comparison between normal and backward readers which takes us that far?

One possible alternative is *the reading level match*. This is a comparison between poor and normal readers of the same reading level. Here, of course, the normal readers must be younger than the poor readers. An example would be a comparison between a group of poor readers of average I.Q. aged 10 years, but with a 7 year reading age; and a group of normal readers aged 7 years, also of average I.Q., with a reading age of 7 years (Fig.5.2).

	Experimental group	Control group
Age	10 years	7 years
I.Q.	100	100
Reading level	7 years	7 years

FIG. 5.2.   Design used in reading level match studies.

This comparison avoids some of the difficulties of the age match. If poor readers prove to be worse than their reading level controls in a phonological task, for example, one can not easily dismiss the difference as the possible product of a difference in reading level, because there is no difference. The two groups are at the same reading level.

So positive results (poor readers performing worse on a given task than their younger reading level controls) in a comparison of this sort are very impressive; but, as we shall see, they are rare. That means that we should also consider what can be concluded from negative results in a reading level comparison (no difference between the two groups) or even positive results in the reverse direction (older poor readers better than the younger normal controls). It is shame to have to say it, but there is very little that one can conclude from such a result.

The trouble is that in these comparisons the poor readers are more advanced intellectually—have a higher mental age—than the normal readers. This may make it possible for the poor readers to conceal a genuine deficit. They may have real difficulties with the skill that the task is designed to test, but end up doing it as well as the other children, because they understand the instructions better or because they know how to attend better. These are extraneous skills which probably improve with age and thus should be stronger in the poor readers than in the children to whom they are being compared. So if no difference is found between the groups, it is not at all clear whether the poor readers have no difficulty or whether they have covered it up with the help of a more sophisticated approach to tasks that adults give them. So positive results in a reading level match deserve a great deal of attention: negative results, in contrast, do not help at all.

Psychologists have used the reading level comparisons quite a lot in work on the significance of phonological skills. They have used three kinds of task: tests of the confusion effect, of rhyme detection and of the ability to read nonsense words.

The Confusion Effect

There is, as we have seen, some dispute about whether Conrad's confusion effect occurs less strongly in backward readers than in other children of the same age. But what would happen in a reading level match? Johnston, Rugg and Scott (1987) answered this question in a study of two groups of backward readers, one aged 8 and the other 11 years old. The experimenters compared these children to normal readers of the same age and also to other normal readers at the same reading level. So the experiment involved both an age and a reading level match. They gave all these children lists of similar and of dissimilar-sounding letters to remember, in much the same way as the Haskins group had done, but they took one extra precaution. When there are large variations in the ages of the children in a memory experiment, you have to make sure that individual children are not being given too much to remember for their age or too little. The experimenters made sure that the task was not altogether too easy or too difficult for each child by finding his or her "memory span" first. Instead of asking all the children to remember the same number of items, they gave each child lists that were one item shorter than that child's span. This was, in fact, a precaution taken by Conrad (1971) in his original developmental study.

The confusion effect, it turned out, was as strong among the poor readers as the normal readers, whether these were matched for age or for reading level. Furthermore, there was no correlation between the size of the effect and the children's performance in a test of reading. In a later study, Holligan and Johnston (1988) repeated these results when they compared an eight year old group of poor readers with normal readers at the same level of reading. In this experiment, too, the confusion effect disappeared in *both* groups of children when they were given lists of letters which exceeded their memory spans.

So the results of the first reading level match study of phonological skills that we report are negative. That does not mean, as we have seen, that the hypothesis that these backward readers suffer from a phonological weakness is wrong.

Explicit Judgements about Rhyme

Rhyme is involved in the confusion effect but only implicitly. But there is also a fair amount of evidence about backward readers' difficulties in tasks in which they have to make explicit judgements about rhyme and about alliteration.

The first study of this sort that we know of was done by Bradley and Bryant (1978). They compared a group of 60 ten year old poor readers who had a reading age of seven and a half years with a group of seven year old normal readers. The children were given a version of the oddity task which was described in the first chapter. They listened to the experimenter saying four words, and then had to say which of the four words had a different sound from the others. In one condition they had to judge which of the four words started with a different sound from the others (e.g. sun, see, sock, *rag*). In two other conditions they had to pick the odd word that ended with a different sound: in one case the vowel sound was different (e.g. *nod*, red, fed, bed), and in the other the final consonant (e.g. weed, *peel*, need, deed). Thus in the first condition—the alliteration task—the children had to make judgements about the words' onsets, and in the other two—the rhyme tasks—about their rimes (Fig.5.3).

The poor readers were worse at recognising the odd word out in all three tasks. They also fared relatively badly in another task in which they had to think of words that rhymed with simple familiar words like "boat", "dog" and "dish". So here is our first

Oddity	Backward readers	Reading–matched group
First sound	2.62	0.67
Middle sound	1.49	0.37
Last sound	1.15	0.17

FIG. 5.3.   Mean errors (out of 6) (Bradley & Bryant, 1978).

example of a positive result and it seems to show a definite phonological problem in backward readers. Backward readers made a large number of mistakes when asked to work out whether different words have common onsets or rimes. They did not do so well even as children whose reading was no better than theirs, children who were three years younger than them. It follows that one cause of their reading problems may be their insensitivity to the speech units, onset and rime.

Other experimenters have come to the same conclusion. Holligan and Johnston (1988) also asked children to read pairs of words and then decide whether they rhymed or not. The poor readers in their study made more mistakes than normal readers with the same reading age. However, not everyone has found the same result. Beech and Harding (1984) compared backward readers both to normal readers of the same reading age and also to others of the same age. They gave the children two rhyme tasks. The poor readers did as well as the children who had the same reading level as them, although a great deal worse than the normal readers of the same age. Once again it is hard to explain this inconsistency. We can only say that it is possible but not certain that an insensitivity to rhyme and alliteration is one of the causes of reading difficulties.

There are further grounds for believing that children who are insensitive to rhyme are as a result likely to become backward readers. Olson et al. (in press; see also Chapter 1) carried out a large-scale study of 117 pairs of twins. At least one child in each pair (the proband) was diagnosed as a backward reader. The experimenters compared these children to younger normal readers at the same reading level as them. The children were given a rhyme production task. They had to think of as many words as they could that rhymed with "eel".

The backward readers were worse, although not much worse, at doing this than the normal readers were. But the most striking results in this study involved "heritability". Because the group of twins included identical and fraternal twins, the experimenters could estimate to what extent the skills being tested were under genetic control. If there is a significant genetic component, the scores of the identical twins should be closer to each other than those of the fraternal twins. The experimenters produced a significant heritability estimate for the twins who were poorest in phonological skills. The monozygotic (genetically identical) twin pairs were almost equally bad at rhyming, whereas the dizygotic probands tended to be much worse than their twin. Olson and his colleagues concluded that: "the underlying causal factor for the disabled readers' heritable phonological coding deficit is a heritable weakness in segmental language skills". It looks as though many backward readers are insensitive to rhyme, and that they may be so for genetic reasons. That makes it even more likely that difficulties with rhyme and alliteration are a cause, and not a result, of reading difficulties.

Reading Nonsense Words

We can only recognise words as familiar patterns if they are familiar. That means that we can use a non-phonological strategy with words that are familiar but not with unfamiliar words. That is one reason why psychologists have used nonsense words like "wef", "dake" or "molsmit" so much. They are bound to be completely unfamiliar to you: therefore you need to use a phonological strategy to read them.

But how does one read "dake" or "molsmit"? One possibility is that you read them letter by letter. Another is that you do it by analogy: you have seen some of the sequences of letters in certain real words (e.g. "cake"), and you simply read these sequences in the same way in the new nonsense word. This is a different strategy but it is still a phonological one, because it depends on associations between certain sounds (usually onset and rime) and certain letter sequences. It is, of course, what Marsh and his colleagues had in mind when they asked people to read words like "biety" and "tepherd".

So people have turned to nonsense words in the search for evidence about the role of phonological awareness, and several of them have compared the ability of poor readers to decipher these words with that of other younger children at the same reading level. Most, but again not all, of these reading level matches have produced a positive result. The backward readers tend to make more mistakes even than the much younger normal children of matched reading levels. We will discuss four studies in some detail.

Frith and Snowling (1983) collected a group of dyslexic children whose reading ages were roughly two years behind their mental ages: their reading age varied from eight years and three months to ten years and nine months. They compared this group to a group of normal children whose reading ages fell within the same range. Frith and Snowling gave these children lists of regular ("coffee", "spade"), irregular ("biscuit", "laugh") and two-syllable nonsense words ("slosbon", "molsmit") to read. They found no difference between the two groups when they read real words, which is not surprising given that the two groups were matched for reading level. However, there was a large difference when it came to nonsense words: the dyslexic children read far fewer of them correctly, and took far longer in their attempts to decipher them.

Similarly, Baddeley, Ellis, Miles and Lewis (1982) compared a group of dyslexic children to a group of younger normal children: both groups had a reading age of 10 years. They gave the children lists of real words and nonsense words to read. The nonsense words were in fact real words changed by single letter (e.g. "dake"). Again, the dyslexic children did as well as the normal children with the real words, but made many more mistakes than the normal children with the nonsense words, and were a lot slower as well.

Other, very similar, studies have produced positive results. One was done by Siegel and Ryan (1988), another by Kochnower, Richardson and DiBenedetto (1983), and a third by Szeszulski and Manis (1987), who found the effect for a group of 10 year old backward readers reading at the 7 year old level. However, there is some inconsistency too. For example, Szezsulski and Manis found the effect in 10 year old but not in 13 year old backward readers, and Treiman and Hirsh-Pasek (1985) did not find it all. In this last study the two experimenters used a reading level match to look at nonsense word reading in a group of 11 year old dyslexic readers who read at the 8 year level. They were compared to a group of eight year old normal readers. Treiman and Hirsh-Pasek found that the children in one group made as many mistakes as those in the other when they were asked to read a list of nonsense words. As in the Baddeley et al. study, the nonsense words were all analogues of real words, which the children were given to read prior to the nonsense word task. So it is difficult to disagree with the authors' conclusion that: "we should not accept uncritically the widespread notion that dyslexics suffer from a specific deficiency in phonological coding..." (p. 363).

Bruck (1988) also failed to find any particular difficulty with nonsense words among a group of backward readers whose ages ranged from 8 to 16 years. These backward readers were as good at reading nonsense words which had been formed by changing one letter of real words (e.g. "goint", "zoor") as were younger children at the same reading level. However, all the backward readers in this study were enrolled in a remediation programme which gave heavy emphasis to phonic skills. So they were receiving extensive drill in the kind of skill which is needed to read nonsense words.

Thus, these studies of children reading nonsense words have not produced entirely consistent results. Nevertheless, other experiments which also involve nonsense words, but which use rather different methods to the ones that we have described, also lead to the conclusion that the claim made by Baddeley et al. and by Snowling and Frith is right.

One of these is a study by Snowling (1980). She gave a matching task to poor readers and to younger children of the same reading age. The experiment involved a series of trials in which two nonsense words were presented, one after the other, and the children had to decide whether they were the same or not. Either these were written words (visual presentation) or they were spoken to the child (auditory presentation). That made four conditions possible. Either both words were written (visual-visual), or they were both spoken (auditory-auditory), or the first was written and the second spoken (visual-auditory) or vice versa (auditory-visual).

There was no difference between the two groups in the first two tasks: the backward readers could match written words with each other, and spoken words with each other, as well as the other children could. But they were worse than normal readers when it came to matching written with spoken words. So backward readers are at a disadvantage when they have to relate sounds to letters, and this is probably because to do so they have to deal with segments of sounds rather than with the sound of the word as a whole.

There is also direct evidence for this idea that backward readers have difficulty with nonsense words because they cannot relate the letters in them to their constituent sounds. Olson, Davidson, Kliegl and Foltz (1985) compared 15 year old disabled readers who had a reading age of 10 years with 10 year old normal readers. The experimenters gave these children pairs of nonsense words like "caik"-"dake", and asked them to say which one sounded like (rhymed with) a real word. They found that the poor readers made significantly more mistakes than the other children did. But there was no difference between the two groups when they were given a written task in which they had to select the real word in a pair of words which sounded exactly the same ("rain", "rane"). So the poor readers had problems with the sounds of nonsense words.

In the same study, Olson and his colleagues asked the children to read nonsense words and found, like Frith and Snowling and also Baddeley et al., that the poor readers made more mistakes than the normal readers did. So this study adds impressively to the evidence that poor readers have particular difficulties with nonsense words, and that the reason for these difficulties is their insensitivity to phonological units. It is worth noting that Olson et al. (in press) gave children the same nonsense words to read in the twin study that we mentioned earlier. The heritability estimate for the children's ability to read nonsense words was also high -almost as high as the estimate for rhyme.

Phonological Difficulties in Some Cases
but not in Others

Keith Stanovich, a research worker with an interest in phonological awareness, has used the reading level match to try to establish that there are two general kinds of backward reader (Stanovich, Nathan & Vala-Rossi, 1986). The two groups are: (1) "garden variety" poor readers; and (2) those with a specific reading retardation which is due to "a specific phonological deficit" (p.280). "Garden variety" poor readers suffer from a general "developmental lag": genuinely dyslexic children, in contrast, suffer from a specific phonological deficit.

As "garden variety poor readers" are behind in everything, including reading, they should not show any particular phonological deficits. We should note that these are not the children that we have been talking about so far in this chapter. So far we have described work on children who have the same I.Q. as the normal readers with whom they are compared. But Stanovich's work draws our attention to children whose intellectual development, as well as their progress in reading, is slow.

Stanovich et al. (1986) tested this hypothesis by comparing 9 and 11 year old children who were either skilled or less-skilled at reading. The skilled 9 year olds and the less-skilled 11 year olds had the same reading level as each other. The children were given a variety of tasks: these were designed to measure their vocabulary, phonological awareness (rhyme production and the oddity tasks), picture and word naming speed (including pseudo-word naming speed) and their use of context. The pattern of the two groups' scores in the different tasks were virtually identical. They were the same even in the phonological tasks. Stanovich et al. concluded that the poor readers had lagged behind in their general development and were not specifically disabled in any way: "Cognitively, they resemble younger children who are at the same stage of reading acquisition" (p. 278).

The experimenters saw the same children again two years later (Stanovich, Nathan & Zolman, 1988). The groups, now aged 11 (skilled) and 13 (less-skilled) respectively, and an 8 year old group matched on reading ability with the 13 year olds, were given a similar battery of tasks. Again, the experimenters met with negative results: the cognitive profiles of the three groups were strikingly similar, although the skilled 11 year olds were now ahead of the 13 year olds in reading. Stanovich et al. (1988) concluded that "the performance of the unlabelled poor reader—that is, those children who read poorly but do not necessarily fit the psychometric criteria for the label reading disabled—will show the cognitive pattern predicted by a developmental lag model...this pattern will contrast with the results from studies where the reading level match involves reading disabled children defined by strict psychometric criteria..." (p.82).

This is, in our view an extremely interesting claim, but it may not be right. The claim is that only children who have a specific reading difficulty and whose other intellectual capacities are normal suffer from a phonological deficit: children whose intellectual development in general, as well as their reading, has fallen behind do not have any particular phonological problem. The idea certainly fits in with the hypothesis that we have been following. However, one still cannot be certain that the group of children whose scores were low in the vocabulary test as well as in the reading test, do not have phonological problems. We argued earlier in this chapter that there is very little to be concluded from a negative result in a reading level match. There are two possible explanations for the fact that Stanovich and his colleagues did not find a difference between the poor and the normal readers. One is that there genuinely is no difference between the two groups on the skills that were tested: that is the experimenters' suggestion. But the alternative is that there might have been a real difference in one or more of these skills, and that it was concealed by the greater sophistication of the backward readers.

Stanovich and his colleagues did consider this second possibility and rejected it on the grounds that the wide range of tasks and the very similar mean performance levels of the two groups made it unlikely. But it seems to us that the frequency of negative results does not make them more convincing or less ambiguous.

Rack (1989) set out to test Stanovich's notion of "garden variety" poor readers. He selected 91 children who fell into two distinct groups. In one, the children's reading levels were well below what would be expected for their age and I.Q.: these were children of average or above average intelligence with relatively low reading levels. The second group consisted of children with relatively low I.Q's: their reading level was also lower than normal for their age, but was in line with their intelligence levels. Rack matched each group with a control group of younger children at the same reading level, whose reading levels were normal for their age. In the experiment the children had to read nonsense words.

Stanovich et al. (1988) would expect that the first of the two groups of backward readers would be worse than their normal control group at reading nonsense words, but that there would be no difference between the second group—definitely a "garden variety" group—and the controls.

The study produced an extremely interesting result. Both groups of backward readers were worse at reading nonsense words than the normal readers to whom they were being compared. So children whose reading levels are low for their chronological age also have phonological difficulties, even when their reading problems could be predicted from their I.Q. One does not have to have a "specific reading difficulty", to use Stanovich's term, to have a phonological problem.

Backward Reading, Backward Spelling

We think it fair to say that reading level matches have produced some impressive evidence that many backward readers are actually held back by an insensitivity to phonological units, such as the phoneme or onset and rime. There are some convincing positive results that point in this direction, and the few negative results do not establish that there is no phonological problem among this group. It is, of course, quite hard to find positive results in a reading level match experiment because the backward readers have a notably higher mental age, and it is worth noting that most positive results that have occurred in this kind of experiment have involved tests of phonological skills. As far as we know, the only other studies to have produced positive results concern children's syntactic and contextual understanding (Guthrie, 1973: Tunmer, Nesdale & Wright, 1986). The hypothesis that phonological difficulties play a crucial role in the difficulties experienced by poor readers is consistent with results from studies which use the reading level match design.

It is time, however, to point to a certain ambiguity in the term "backward readers". Backward readers are almost without exception backward spellers as well. Occasionally adults who suffer from some form of brain damage seem unable to read and yet they can spell words reasonably well. But one does not find that pattern among children. When we compare "backward readers" with normal readers we are also looking at a group whose spelling is very poor. So it would make just as much sense to say, when we find a positive result in a reading level match, that we have found out something about the causes of spelling difficulties as of reading difficulties. But this is quite embarrassing because, as we have already shown, there is evidence that children learn to read and spell in rather different ways.

The problem seems all the more pressing when it emerges that groups matched in terms of one skill are rather different in terms of the other. The backward readers in Bradley and Bryant's (1978) study had the same reading age as the normal children, but they actually had a lower spelling age on average than the children in the normal group. So one could argue that their difficulties in rhyme might be the result of a difference in spelling levels. This seems unlikely because the difference in spelling levels was really quite small, but the possibility cannot be ruled out.

Of course, one can match groups on spelling levels rather than on their reading levels, and this seems to us to be a wise move when the experiment is on a topic which is obviously more relevant to spelling than to reading. We know of two studies with a spelling level match.

Rohl and Tunmer (1988) wanted to test the hypothesis of a strong connection between children's awareness of phonemes and their spelling. They compared three groups of children, all of whom had reached the same level in a standardised spelling test. This was the level typical of the average child of eight years. The children in one group (the "good" group) were only seven years and three months in age; in another group (the "average" group) just eight years old; and in the third (the "poor" group) ten years and four months. The intellectual levels of the children in the three groups were around average for their age.

Rohl and Tunmer's measure of the children's sensitivity to phonemes was a phoneme tapping task. The words which the children had to tap were nonsense words, and they varied in length—from two to five phonemes. The words' length turned out to be important. There was not much difference between the groups when they had to tap the two-phoneme words, but as the number of phonemes in the words increased so did the difference between the groups. The poor spellers were much worse than the others at tapping out the phonemes in the longer words.

This is an interesting result, and it suggests that children's sensitivity to phonemes is important to them when they learn to spell. But we do not know whether it is just a question of phonemes (would the poor spellers have been just as bad in a syllable task, or in a task involving judgements about onset and rime?), and we cannot be sure that the study establishes a direct connection between the phonological test and spelling. After all, the poor spellers were probably poor readers too.

We have the same worry about our second example of a spelling level match. This was made in the study by Bruck and Treiman (1989) described in Chapter 3. This was an experiment in which seven year old children had to say which words contained particular consonants. In another task, a deletion task, they had to work out what a word would sound like if a consonant was removed from it. These seven year olds found both tasks much harder when the consonant was only part of the onset (in a CCV word) than when it was the entire onset (in a CVC word).

We have come back to this study because it also involved another group of children who were poor spellers. They were 10 year old children who read at the level of a typical child of 7 years. Bruck and Treiman had two things to report about the poor spellers. The first was that their scores in the recognition and deletion tasks were lower in general than those of the seven year old children: the second is that, nevertheless, they experienced exactly the same pattern of difficulties: they too found the CCV words much harder to disentangle than the CVC ones.

Here is more evidence that children with spelling problems experience phonological difficulties which are unusually great even for the spelling level that they have managed to reach. But of course we encounter the same ambiguity as we did with the Rohl and Tunmer study. The backward spellers were backward at reading as well (Bruck and Treiman report the reading levels for the 10 year old children, and these were also very low) and so we cannot be sure of a direct connection between the children's phonological skills and their spelling.

There is a way to make this distinction. Backward readers may invariably be bad at spelling too, but there are plenty of children and adults who can read perfectly well but are hopeless at spelling.

POOR SPELLERS AND THE PHONOLOGICAL CODE

Uta Frith (1980) introduced the idea of looking at children who spell poorly, but have no particular difficulty with reading. She decided to compare them to children who have fallen behind both in reading and in spelling, as well as to others who have neither kind of difficulty.

In her initial study she compared three groups of 12 year old children: (1) good readers and good spellers; (2) good readers and poor spellers; (3) poor readers and poor spellers. The first thing that she did was to give them a spelling task (the Schonell Graded Word Spelling Test, Schonell & Goodacre, 1971), in order to look at the kind of mistakes that the children made. She categorised the mistakes either as *phonetic* because they preserved sound (e.g. "coff" for "cough", "surch" for "search"); or as *non-phonetic* because they were unrelated to sound (e.g. "couge" for "cough", "suach" for "search").

Frith found that the mistakes made by the discrepant group—those who were poor spellers but good readers—were mainly phonetic. The children who were good at reading and at spelling made fewer mistakes, but these too were also mainly phonetic. The children, in contrast to the other two groups, who were poor at spelling and at reading, made as many non-phonetic as they did phonetic mistakes.

What does this pattern tell us? Frith concluded that the discrepant group—poor at spelling but good at reading—could use letter-sound correspondence rules, but often selected the wrong ones. They tried to retain the correct sound of a word, and in fact were quite consistent in the kinds of misspellings which they produced: 41% of their misspellings were identical when they were tested with the same list a few weeks later. In contrast, the poor spellers who were also poor at reading did not seem to be able to use letter-sound correspondence rules nearly so well, and only 23% of their misspellings were consistent at re-test a few weeks later. Thus the discrepant group adopted a phonological strategy, but even so were unable to spell at the level predicted by their reading ability.

Frith also asked the children to write nonsense words in order to check whether the phonological skills of the children in the discrepant group were intact. These nonsense words were derived from real English words [e.g. "usterand" (understand), "rekind" (remind)]. Again the two groups of good readers (those who were good at reading and spelling and those who were poor at spelling but good at reading) produced significantly more phonetically acceptable spellings than the poor readers.

If the children in the discrepant group use phonological rules so assiduously, why are they such bad spellers? One obvious possibility is that they cannot remember what written words look like and therefore are unable to remember exception words ("ache") at all well or to select the right spelling pattern for a particular word ("beef" vs. "beaf"). In that case, Frith argued, they should be able to read misspelled words which "sound correct" such as "nite" and "clime" more easily than ones which sound wrong, but look rather like the correct form, such as "nght" and "clmb". So she designed passages of prose for the three groups to read: there were two types of passage: one contained many misspelled words of the "sounds right" kind, the other of the "looks right" kind. She expected the children in the discrepant group to do a great deal better with the first type of passage than with the second.

In fact the opposite happened. The children in that group had very great difficulty with the "sounds right" words, and yet coped with the "looks right" words quite easily. It was the children in the other two groups who managed better in the "sounds right" condition than in the "looks right" one. How does one explain this unexpected result? Frith's explanation is particularly interesting as far as this book is concerned, because she argued that the discrepant group read in one way (visually) and spell in another (phonologically). So her hypothesis about these particular 12 year olds is similar to the argument that we have developed about 6 and 7 year old children in general. Perhaps the children who become poor spellers but good readers never abandon an approach to reading and spelling which most children drop by the age of eight years or so.

There are signs however that Frith's results may not hold for younger children. Waters et al. (1985) set out to replicate Frith's 1980 study with three groups of eight year old children: good readers and good spellers, good readers and poor spellers, and poor readers and poor spellers. They found that the discrepant group (good readers but poor spellers) made significantly fewer phonetically accurate misspellings than the good group (good readers and good spellers), whereas in Frith's study the mixed group made almost as many phonetically acceptable misspellings as the good group. The discrepant group and the group of poor readers and poor spellers made the same proportion of phonetically accurate misspellings.

However, Waters et al. used a more stringent system than Frith for classifying spelling mistakes as phonetically inaccurate. They classified spellings such as "natcher" for "nature", "educat" for "educate" and "magority" for "majority" as phonetically inaccurate, even though there is clear evidence of a phonological basis for these spellings. This may explain their failure to replicate Frith's result.

Bruck and Waters (1988) compared the performance of groups of good, discrepant and poor spellers, aged eight and eleven years, in a standardised test of spelling. They analysed the children's mistakes using two classification systems, one lenient and the other stringent. The lenient "unconstrained" system allowed misspellings such as "natcher" and "magority" to be counted as phonetically accurate, while the stringent "constrained" system rejected these mistakes but allowed misspellings such as "naicher" and "mijourity". Bruck and Waters found that they repeated Frith's results, but with the older group only and only with the more lenient system for classifying errors. We can still accept Frith's interesting claim about older children—that children who spell poorly but read well do so because they have not made as effective a connection between reading and spelling as other children have.

Spelling versus Reading

All of these studies of poor spellers support the idea that the phonological code plays a crucial role in spelling. Perhaps this kind of research can tell us something about another theme of this book, which has been that the phonological strategy is more important in spelling than in reading. An experiment by Perin (1983) certainly supports this idea.

She looked at three groups of 14 and 15 year olds: these groups were exactly like the three in Frith's study. Group A read and spelled well, Group B (the discrepant group) read well but spelled poorly, and Group C both read and spelled poorly. Perin gave these children two different tests of phonological awareness. The first was a Spoonerism test in which the children were given a series of names of pop stars, and had to swop the initial consonants of the two names (e.g. Chuck Berry to Buck Cherry). In the second the children had to judge the number of phonemes in some words.

Perin found that the children's spelling levels and not their reading levels determined how well they did. In both tasks Group A did a great deal better than the other two groups. Perin also analysed the pattern of the mistakes that children made. Seventy per cent or more of the mistakes in each group were phonemic in nature. One common mistake was to repeat the initial consonant of the second part of the name (Dob Dylan for Dob Bylan); another was to substitute too many phonemes (Beck Chunk for Buck Cherry). The poor spellers were therefore able to segment phonemes, but often transposed them wrongly.

We cannot tell what is cause and what effect here. The poor spellers may be less skilled with phonemes because their knowledge of spelling is faulty. Or their spelling may have fallen behind because of their insensitivity with phonemes. But whatever the direction of cause and effect, Perin's result does suggest that phonological awareness continues to be important as spelling develops.

CONCLUSIONS

Children who make slow progress in reading and spelling often have phonological problems, even in comparison to children who have reached the same absolute level of reading or spelling. This is certainly evidence for a causal connection between children's phonological skills and their success (or lack of it) in reading and spelling, but it is not conclusive evidence. There may be factors that govern the reading of the 5% or so of children who are dyslexic that play no part in the reading of normal children. So we have to turn to studies of normal readers to see whether the effects that we have discussed in this chapter are representative ones. This takes us to the next chapter.

CHAPTER 6

Correlations and Longitudinal Predictions

THE NEED FOR CORRELATIONS

Another way to look at causal connections is to search for relations between different skills. If children's awareness of sounds does play a part in their reading, we should be able to find a relation between their success in phonological tasks and the progress that they make in learning to read. The more sensitive children are to the sounds in words, the better they should be at reading.

Of course, a simple relation of that sort on its own is not very convincing. You would almost certainly find a correlation between children's scores in any phonological task and their success in a reading test, even if there were no connection at all between these two skills. That is because bright children would probably do better than the others in both tests and children who are not so advanced in general would do badly in both. In that case the correlation between phonological skills and reading would be quite spurious: the two would only be related because both are determined by the same third factor, the children's intelligence.

So, when one looks for an uncontaminated relationship between children's phonological abilities and their success in learning to read, one has to control for differences in extraneous variables such as the children's intelligence, their verbal knowledge and if possible their social background too. As we shall see later, this is quite easy to do.

But that is not all. We also have to show that the relationship is a specific one. The idea that we have been pursuing is that children's sensitivity to sounds affects their success in reading by helping them to understand the relationships between letters and sounds. Therefore we are looking at the evidence for (and against) a specific link between a particular linguistic skill and a particular educational achievement. There is every reason according to our hypothesis why phonological skills should be related to reading: there is no reason why they should be related to, for example, children's understanding of mathematics. That means that we ought to show that children's phonological skills are related to reading and *not* to their mathematical skills. Otherwise we run the risk of simply finding a variable which is related to educational achievement in general.

Suppose that we do establish an uncontaminated and a specific correlation between children's phonological acumen and their success in reading. What claims can we make on the basis of this result?

The first thing to note is that we need the result badly. Anyone who tries to show a connection between phonological skills and reading should be able to demonstrate a specific correlation between the two. We should have to abandon the hypothesis if this correlation did not exist. We could not say that one skill leads to the other in the face of evidence that it makes no difference to a child's success in reading whether she is extremely good or extremely bad at dissecting the sounds in words.

So evidence for a specific correlation between the two skills is another minimum requirement, and that is why this evidence is so important. Nevertheless, on its own a correlation can never prove the existence of a causal connection. Correlations show us where such connections might exist, and they also warn us about causal connections which definitely do not exist. But they do not by themselves establish cause and effect.

TWO KINDS OF CORRELATION

Before we discuss the limitations of the correlation, we must make a distinction between different kinds of correlation. One kind is a correlation between children's scores in two tasks that they have been given roughly at the same time. You give a group of six year olds, for example, a number of tests, and then you look at the correlations between the different scores. The second type is the longitudinal relation. Here one measure is taken quite some time before the other: you measure a particular skill in a group of children when they are three years, and then two years later when they are five you measure another skill. The question is whether the children's scores on the first occasion are related to, and thus predict, how well they do in the task that they are given two years later.

We make this distinction because one can draw different conclusions from the two kinds of correlation. The first kind of correlation—the simultaneous correlation—simply tells us that a relation exists and nothing else. You cannot tell anything about the direction of cause and effect. Suppose that one does find a correlation between children's scores in a phonological task and the way that they read. That could mean that children's phonological skills determine their progress in reading, or alternatively that their progress in reading affects their phonological awareness.

There is another limitation to this kind of correlation. It is the problem of the unknown third factor which we have touched on already. There is always the danger that both measures might be affected by some other unknown, and therefore unmeasured, third factor, and thus that despite a positive correlation there may be no connection between the two. The positive correlation might be spurious. Of course one should take all possible steps to control for the obvious other factors that we do know about, and should control for differences in these.

The difference with longitudinal correlations is that they suffer only one of these two limitations. There is no problem about direction, for example, in longitudinal predictions of reading. You measure the skill that you are interested in before the children have begun to read, and then years later you relate these original scores to their success in learning to read. If you find a predictive relation, there is no question of the children's experiences with reading having any effect on the original measure of the skill that interests you because they had not begun to read when that measure was taken. However, you can never avoid the problem of the unknown third factor. That is why neither kind of correlation on its own can finally establish a causal connection. But both, as we shall see, have produced valuable information about phonological awareness and reading.

PHONOLOGICAL UNITS AND THE TWO TYPES OF CORRELATION

It follows from what we have just said that longitudinal correlations should be much more help to us than simultaneous ones are. Longitudinal predictions of reading are particularly valuable when the first measure is taken before children begin to learn to read. But this means that it will be much easier to use some phonological measures than others in a longitudinal prediction of this sort. As we have seen (Chapter 1), children manage some phonological tests quite well long before they can read, but others are only possible for them either at around the time they begin to read or several years after. They can do well in tests of rhyme long before they begin to read, but they only begin to tap out phonemes at about the age when they are beginning to read, and some forms of the deletion and elision test (Bruce's for example) are far too hard for them as long as two years after they have begun to read.

We can, of course, look at the relations between all these tests and the way in which children learn to read. But longitudinal predictions in which the first measure is taken before the children have had any experience with reading will only be possible with phonological tests like the rhyme tests which children can manage when they are three or four years old.

SIMULTANEOUS CORRELATIONS AND THE DETECTION OF PHONEMES

We claimed in Chapter 2 that young children do not use grapheme-phoneme correspondences much when they are beginning to learn to read: we argued that the children depend instead on the larger phonological units of onset and rime when they make connections between sounds and letters. If this is right, there is no particular reason to expect a relation between children's sensitivity to phonemes and their success in reading, at any rate during their first few years at school.

One of the reasons that we gave for thinking that phonemes play a relatively insignificant role in the early stages of reading was that young children are strikingly insensitive to phonemes. Tasks in which they have to detect or manipulate phonemes are extremely difficult, and sometimes impossible, for them. The difficulty of phoneme tasks has another consequence. It means that it is extremely hard to do a longitudinal study in which children are given a measure of phoneme detection before they learn to read. Children who have not begun to read usually cannot cope with such tasks. Therefore, most of the correlational data on sensitivity to phonemes and reading is not longitudinal in the sense that we have used the word. So correlations between these measures and reading are bound to be unsatisfactory because they do not allow us to be definite about the direction of cause and effect.

1. Working out how many Phonemes there are in a Word: One-to-One Correspondence

One way of testing children's awareness of the phonemes in words, as we have seen (Chapter 1), is to ask them to act out in some way the number of phonemes in a word. The usual way that this is done is for children to lay out one brick or counter or to tap once for each phoneme. This is actually quite difficult for young children, and on the whole they cannot cope with such tests until after they have begun to read. Several people have tried to make a connection between children's performance in this kind of task and their reading skills.

We shall begin with a claim by Calfee, P. Lindamood and C. Lindamood (1973) that there is a relation between children's ability to judge how many phonemes a word contains and their reading. Theirs was a large-scale study of 660 schoolchildren. The experimenters gave the children, whose ages ranged between 6 and 18 years, a task (the Lindamood Auditory Conceptualisation Test) in which they had to arrange coloured blocks to represent sounds. The sounds were either "discrete" like s-s-n, or "integrated" units like "ips". Notice that only the "integrated" units test children's ability to separate out the constituent sounds in a word.

The children found it more difficult to represent the integrated than the discrete units, as one would expect. Their scores in this test were related to their reading skills and to their spelling as well. But here is an obvious example of the ambiguity of a simple correlation. We cannot tell whether the children's experiences with reading had affected their ability to detect phonemes, as the Brussels group would claim, or whether the connection went in the other direction. There is an even more serious problem about this study. The authors measured the children's I.Q. but did not control for I.Q. differences when they related the scores on their test of phoneme detection to reading. The children who did well in Calfee et al.'s test may have been the cleverer children who, just because they were cleverer, were also to become successful readers. So the correlation could simply have been a product of I.Q. differences and thus an entirely spurious one.

Liberman et al. (1974) looked for a correlation between their phoneme tapping task and children's reading. They reported that those children who had had most difficulty with that task made least progress in reading. However, here we meet again the same two problems that made the Calfee et al. study so ambiguous. Differences in I.Q. were not controlled, and we cannot be sure about the causal direction. In fact, the strong improvement in this phoneme tapping task between the ages of five and six years when the children began to read (see Chapter 1) suggests that phoneme segmentation benefits from reading instruction.

Cossu, Shankweiler, Liberman, Tola and Katz, (1987) gave Italian children the tasks that were originally used in the Liberman et al. study. These experimenters found the same difference between syllable and phoneme tapping (the phoneme tapping task is harder) in Italian pre-schoolers, and they also found that the children improved rapidly in the phoneme task when they first went to school (first grade). The school children in the study were seven and eight years old. The experimenters then divided them into good, average and poor readers. The poor readers made the most errors in the phoneme task. Cossu et al. (1987) concluded that children's ability to detect phonemes is related to their progress in reading. This ability distinguished children of different levels of reading skill. But, again, the difference between the groups could simply have been a matter of I.Q. There is little evidence here for any direct connection between children's awareness of phonemes and their success in reading.

Thus far the evidence about the connection is ambiguous, and our doubts are further bolstered by some of the results of the Treiman and Baron (1981) study which we mentioned in Chapter 1, where we described how they asked children to put down a counter for each phoneme or syllable in words spoken by the experimenter. Treiman and Baron found that reading (as measured by the Wide Range Achievement Test) did not correlate with performance in the phoneme counting task, but that there was a correlation between the children's reading and their performance in the syllable counting task. Again, the link between phoneme detection and reading seems an improbable one.

However, the results of one imaginative and well-conducted study force us to think again about this connection. Tunmer and Nesdale (1985) looked at the relationship between children's success in a phoneme tapping task and their scores in a reading test. The study involved 63 six year old children, who were given the task of tapping out the number of phonemes in real and nonsense words. Some of these words contained digraphs (two letters representing one sound, like "oo" in "book"). Others (e.g. "man") did not. The authors also included a measure of the children's intellectual levels. This was a vocabulary test (the P.P.V.T.) which correlates well with I.Q. Lastly, the experimenters tested the children's reading skills in a standardised test of reading and in a task in which they were given a list of nonsense words to read.

Tunmer and Nesdale found a strong relationship between the children's success in the non-digraph phoneme tapping test and their reading and, more to the point, this relation was still significant when differences in the children's intellectual levels had been controlled. So here for the first time we meet convincing evidence of a specific relation between children's sensitivity to phonemes and the progress that they make in reading, and it is worth spending a little time considering how the authors did manage to control for intellectual differences.

They did so in a "fixed order" multiple regression. The aim of this kind of statistical analysis is to find out how much of the variation in one set of scores can be accounted for by other variables. In this case, the authors wanted to know how much of the variance in the children's reading scores could be accounted for by the children's vocabulary scores and by their performance in the phoneme tapping task. The first step that they took in this analysis was to see how much of this variance was explained by variations in the children's vocabulary. Their vocabulary scores accounted for a fair amount of the variance in the children's reading score. The second step was to see how much of the "remaining" variance in the reading scores was explained by the differences in the children's phoneme tapping skills. In fact the phoneme tapping scores accounted for 21% of the variance in reading—a very striking and, of course, a highly significant relationship.

But the most important thing to realise is that this was the strength of the relationship between the phoneme tapping scores and reading *after* the effects of differences in vocabulary had been controlled. By entering vocabulary as the first step in this multiple regression the authors had ensured that any relationship between a variable entered as a following step would be independent of differences in vocabulary. That is the way to make sure that a relationship is specific and to rule out the effects of differences in extraneous variables—or at any rate the extraneous variables that one knows about.

Thus, Tunmer and Nesdale established a genuinely specific relationship between children's ability to detect phonemes and their success in reading. But, of course, the direction of cause and effect in this study remains an open question. It is at least as possible that the children's experiences in reading determined their performance in the tapping task as the other way round. In fact the results of another part of the study fit well with this second idea—that children's experiences with reading have a strong effect on how they set about detecting phonemes. The children tended to tap once too often to words, like "book", with digraphs (see Chapter 1). So a child would typically tap three times to "man" but four times to "book". Yet both are three-phoneme words. The most convincing explanation for the surplus of taps to the digraph words was that the children were tapping the letters, not the sounds, in the word. In that case the knowledge that they have gained from learning to read controls their ability to detect phonemes rather than the other way round.

Thus, the most convincing demonstration that we have of a specific relationship between children's ability to detect phonemes (as measured by the phoneme tapping task) in the end leads to the suggestion that sensitivity to phonemes depends on children's experience of learning to read rather than the other way round. There is no evidence from any of these experiments that children's sensitivity to phonemes determines how well they read.

2. Deletion Studies

Another way of testing children's sensitivity to phonemes is to ask them to work out what a word would sound like if a sound were removed from it. We saw several studies of children's ability to do this in Chapter 1. Two of them also included measures of the children's success in reading and correlations between the children's reading levels and their performance in the phoneme deletion task.

Fox and Routh (1975), you will remember, asked children to "say just a little bit..." of a word. They reported a significant correlation between the children's scores in a standardised test of reading and their performance in the trials in which they had to delete phonemes. However, these experimenters say nothing about controlling for differences in I.Q., and so we cannot be sure that there is a genuine connection between these two sets of scores.

The second of the two studies is Rosner and Simon's (1971). They also reported a positive correlation between the children's success in the deletion task ("lend-end", "belt-bel") and their reading levels. But this was a much more impressive result because these authors did control for differences in I.Q. So this time it looks as though there was a specific connection. However, in the phonological test the children had to delete phonemes ("lend-end", "pray-ray", "belt-bel", "stream-steam") in some trials, and syllables ("carpet-car", "reproduce-reduce", "location-lotion") in others. This was not a pure measure of phoneme detection, and so we still have no clear evidence that sensitivity to phonemes plays a part in learning to read.

3. Relations between Different measures of Phonological Awareness

It seems to us that psychologists resorted to simultaneous correlations with measures of phoneme awareness because they had no choice. They could not run longitudinal studies, which would have been much more satisfactory, with these measures for the reasons that we have already given. In contrast people who have worked with phonological tasks, such as rhyme tasks, which children can manage before they learn to read have tended to look for longitudinal relationships. There are several studies, as we shall see, in which the experimenter has given children rhyme and alliteration tasks before they begin to learn to read and then has related their scores in these tasks to the progress that they make later on in reading.

However, there are also some studies in which children are given measures of phoneme detection as well as of awareness of rhyme, and in these the measures perforce had to be administered to children who had already begun to read.

Some authors have given several tests of awareness of phonemes to the same children. Yopp (1988) did one of the most interesting studies of this type. She worked with children whose age ranged from five years and four months to six years and eight months, and included tests of phoneme tapping, phoneme blending and phoneme deletion. She also gave the children a rhyme test: the children heard a series of pairs of words: sometimes the words in the pair rhymed with each other and sometimes not.

Yopp also tried a test of phoneme reversal like the one developed by Morais and his colleagues (Chapter 1), but she was forced to abandon it because it proved too difficult for the children.

Yopp tried to test the children's reading ability, but her test was a curious one. The children had to learn to read nonsense words like "hof", "dap" and "gos", and Yopp makes it clear that she taught these words by telling the children about the grapheme-phoneme correspondences. "I pointed to each letter as I said its sound. After saying each sound, I blended the sounds together to form the word" (p. 167). The measure of "reading acquisition" was how quickly the children learned these nonsense words. It should be said straightaway that this is not a test of reading ability: it is a test of the child's ability to learn to use grapheme-phoneme rules, which is quite another matter. Of course one would expect children's performance in phoneme detection tasks to be closely related to this kind of "reading", but one should have no confidence at all that the scores in this test have anything to do with the way that children read real words.

Not surprisingly, Yopp found that the children's scores in the phoneme detection tests were related to their performance in her reading test. So were their scores in the rhyme test, but not so strongly. This difference is also unsurprising: rhyme involves larger phonological units than the phoneme, and the reading test was so firmly rooted in phonemes.

Yopp made another claim about the relative significance of children's awareness of rhyme and of phonemes. She carried out a factor analysis and reported that the children's scores in the different tests of phoneme detection were strongly related to each other, which meant that the tests seemed to be testing the same thing. However, the rhyme scores were out on a limb in this factor analysis. Yopp writes: "Rhyming ability is only minimally involved in these factors. Rhyme tasks may tap a different underlying ability than other tests of phonemic awareness. Therefore generalisations about phonemic awareness drawn from research which focuses on rhyme tasks should be considered with caution" (p.172). Here, Yopp seems to be saying two things. One is that rhyme scores are not closely related to phoneme detection scores, and the other is that one should therefore be cautious about rhyme.

It seems to us that the result—phoneme detection tests more closely related to each other than to rhyme—is important because it establishes what we have been suggesting all along, that awareness of phonological speech units like onset and rime and awareness of phonemes are separate skills (which children acquire at different stages of development). But that does not mean that rhyme is unimportant, as Yopp seems to be suggesting. True, the rhyme scores were not so strongly related to her reading test (although the correlation of 0.47 does not seem too bad to us), but the "reading" test was a test of learning about phonemes and therefore not a proper test of reading. Yopp also misleads her readers when she warns them against drawing conclusions about "phonemic awareness" from rhyme tasks. No one is suggesting that one should. "Phonemic awareness" means awareness of phonemes. But rhyme, as we have repeatedly pointed out, involves the speech unit, rime, and not the phoneme.

Rhyme would be unimportant if reading were just a matter of grapheme-phoneme conversion, but that is certainly not the case. Even the close relationship that Yopp reported between the children's performance in the phoneme detection tasks and their learning scores in her "reading" task should be treated with some caution because there were no measures of I.Q. in her study, and it is quite likely that the children's performance in both tasks was heavily influenced by their intelligence. Thus this study, like so many of the other studies that we have described so far, does not establish a specific connection between children's awareness of phonemes and the progress that they make in learning to read.

LONGITUDINAL STUDIES AND THE DETECTION OF PHONEMES

One can, of course, start a longitudinal study with children of any age. But longitudinal studies of children's reading are much more impressive if the children are given the first measures long before they can read than if the study starts when they have begun to read already. That requirement, as we have already remarked, is a nuisance when it comes to phoneme detection tests which children who are young enough to be pre-readers usually find impossibly difficult.

However, some people have tried to do longitudinal studies with these tests. On the whole, in our view, these studies start too late—when the children have just arrived at school or have been there for some time. Children as old as this may already read to some extent, and in fact in some studies it is clear that those taking part knew a great deal about reading by the time the first measures were taken. Thus, one of the main advantages of the longitudinal study—that of being certain of the direction of cause and effect—is often lost.

Short-term Studies

We shall start with some studies which lasted over so short a period—usually over only one year—that they are not very different from investigations which involve simultaneous correlations. In these short-term studies the children are usually seen when they first come to school and then again at the end of their first year there.

This was the pattern of a comprehensive and extremely useful study by Stanovich, Cunningham and Cramer (1984). They worked with a group of six year old children and they gave them eight different tests of phoneme detection as well two tests of rhyme. The children's scores in the phoneme tests correlated extremely well with each other and yet they were on the face of it a rather heterogeneous bunch of tests. The children had to work out whether the initial and the final consonants of different words were the same; they had to delete a phoneme; they had to substitute one phoneme for another in a word; they had to say which word did not share a particular consonant with three others; and they had to say what was the phoneme which one word possessed and another lacked ("cat", "at"). Despite the considerable differences in the form of these tasks, they correlated well with each other. It is a pity that the authors did not control for differences in intelligence (which they had measured) when they ran these correlations, because it is quite possible that some of the apparent connections between the different phoneme detection tests could simply have been the result of differences in intelligence. But the correlations are so large that it seems unlikely to us that they could be completely explained in this way.

The rhyme tests were too easy for the children, and did not really tell them apart. As a result the children's scores in these tests were not related to their performance in the phoneme tests or to their reading. (In fact, a very similar study by Stuart and M. Coltheart, 1988, with younger children demonstrates that when rhyme tests are not too easy they do correlate with phoneme tests. We will come back to this study later on.)

We put Stanovich, Cunningham and Cramer's study into our "short-term longitudinal" section because a year after these phonological tests were administered, the experimenters gave a reading test to some of the same children. They found that there was a strong relation between these children's performance in the initial phoneme detection tasks and the progress that they had made in reading a year later on. But it seems that the authors did not do enough to control for differences in I.Q. here either. Quite rightly, they did a multiple regression, but (and this is important) they did not enter I.Q. into the regression before entering the phoneme detection scores. You can only be sure that such scores predict reading in a multiple regression if you put I.Q. into the regression first and then the phonological scores.

We are afraid that this lack of caution about I.Q.—this tendency not to rule out the possibility that the relation between the ability of young children to detect phonemes and reading was caused by I.Q.—pervades most of the work that we are about to describe in the rest of this section on short-term longitudinal studies.

Calfee (1977), for example, found that his deletion test ("pies"-"eyes") which we described in Chapter 1 predicted children's reading a year later quite well, but he does not seem to have controlled for differences in I.Q. Nor did Mann (1984) rule out the effects of differences in intelligence in an otherwise excellent study. She gave some six year old children two tasks: in one they had to reverse the order of the syllables in two- or three-syllable nonsense words, in another to reverse the order of phonemes in two-phoneme words. She also tested their reading levels a year later when they were seven years old. The phoneme reversal task was of course much the harder of the two, and it also proved to be a much better predictor of reading. (The reason for this last result could have been that the syllable reversal task was so easy that it did not really tell the children apart.) In fact, the children's scores on the phoneme reversal task were a very good predictor of their reading scores a year later. But we simply cannot tell how much of this relationship was simply due to differences in the children's I.Q.s. Although Mann did do multiple regressions, she, like Stanovich and his colleagues, did not use them to remove the effects of differences in I.Q. She did not enter I.Q. as a step in the multiple regressions before putting her phonological measures into the analysis.

Our final example is an ingenious study which involves children's awareness of phonemes, their progress in reading and also the method by which they are taught. This was a year-long study by Perfetti, Beck, Bell and Hughes (1987) [which is also described in Perfetti's interesting book (1985)]. The children studied were six and seven years old and already at school when the study started. These children were at two different schools, which had adopted different methods of teaching reading. In one school the reading programme was based on the "whole-word" method and in the other on "phonics".

Perfetti and his colleagues were interested in the possibility of a difference between segmenting (breaking words up into phonemes) and blending (constructing a word from phonemes), and they also wanted to know whether the different ways of teaching these children to read affected their progress in reading. So they gave the children segmenting and blending tests at different points in this year-long study, and they tested the children's ability to read nonsense words on these occasions as well. The blending test required the children to put together sounds spoken by the experimenter into a word ("m-a-n"-"man"). The segmentation tests were of two kinds. One was the tapping task used by Liberman et al. (1974) and the other required the children to delete the initial ("cat"-"at") or the final ("cat"-"ca") sound in words. Thus, the former task requires phonemic segmentation, whereas the latter is partially based on onset-rime units.

The experimenters reported that the children's scores in the deletion task were those most strongly related to their performance in a standardised test of reading given a year later, and this relationship held at all testing points in the year for both groups. In contrast, the phonemic (tapping) segmentation task and the blending task were only significantly related to reading for the whole word group. Thus, the only consistent predictors were those that partially involved the units onset and rime. The authors also report predictive relationships between their measures and performance in the nonsense word reading task. However, nonsense word reading is different from real reading, and while their conclusions are extremely interesting, they did not do nearly enough to control for the effects of differences in I.Q.—even though they did measure I.Q. in their study.

All of the studies that we have described in this section have produced strong relations between the children's success in tests of phoneme awareness and their progress in reading a little later on. But none of them really establishes that there is a genuine connection here. This is a pity because a lot depends on the question. One needs to know whether there is a specific connection between phoneme detection and reading because of the hypothesis, for which we have gathered quite a lot of evidence (Chapter 2), that awareness of phonemes plays little part in the early stages of reading.

We also argued (Chapter 3) that children's awareness of phonemes plays a much more important part in children's spelling than in their reading. Yet the studies that we have dealt with so far have stuck to measures of children's reading, and thus do not tell us all that we need to know. Luckily, as we shall see in the next section, there are longitudinal studies which have the proper controls for extraneous variables and which do contain measures of spelling as well as of reading.

STUDIES OVER LONGER TIME PERIODS

For some reason people doing longitudinal studies which cover long periods of time have come closest to solving the empirical problems that we have been worrying about in previous sections in this chapter. These people have produced convincing evidence for a connection between children's phonological skills and their reading which is genuine and specific. It is not clear why research of this particular genre should have managed so well, but it deserves a lot of attention. To make this point we start our account of long-term longitudinal studies with a description of three European studies which have produced strong evidence for the relation between phonological skills and children's reading.

1. Phonological Skills and Reading Two Years Later—a Swedish Study

The first is a large-scale study carried out in Sweden by Lundberg, Olofsson and Wall (1980). Their aim was to see whether the phonological skills that children possess before they go to school are related to their success in learning to read and spell later on. The project started with the experimenters giving a large number of kindergarten children a set of linguistic tasks. The children involved were six and seven years old at the time (one thing to note here is that in Sweden children do not go to school until quite late).

In the initial task Lundberg et al. asked the children to break words up either into their component syllables or into their component phonemes, and also to work out what words were formed when they were given these words' syllables or phonemes. As well as this the children were given a task called the "analysis of phoneme position test". Here they had to say whether a particular phoneme such as /s/ came at the beginning or in the middle or at the end of words read out to them. This task could be used to look at children's sensitivity to onset and rime (and indeed Bruck and Treiman in the study that we have already described did use a variant of this task to do that), but the experimenters were not interested in the onset-rime distinction. Finally, the experimenters asked the children to think up words that rhymed with words given them by the experimenter.

One year later the children, who were now at school, were seen again and the experimenters measured their progress in reading and spelling and also gave them a non-verbal intelligence test (the Raven's). A year after that the experimenters tested most of the children's reading and spelling for the second time.

When Lundberg and his colleagues looked at the pattern of relations between the initial tests and the children's reading a year later they were faced with an embarrassment of riches. The children's scores in very nearly all of the initial tests of their ability to detect and manipulate syllables and phonemes were related to their reading skills at the end of their first year at school (even when the effects of differences in I.Q. were controlled), and so was the original rhyme production test. This certainly suggests a connection between phonological awareness and reading, but it does not tell us anything about the nature of this connection.

In contrast, only two of the initial tests were related to the children's reading scores two years later, the second time that they were seen at school. These were the children's rhyme scores and their scores in the "analysis of phoneme position test". What does this mean?

One of these successful tests (rhyme production) involved detection and production of rimes, and the other (analysis of phoneme position) the recognition of phonemes which sometimes coincided with the word's onset and sometimes did not. So the fact that these two tests were the successful predictors certainly establishes that the awareness that children have of onset and rime before they go to school is connected to their success in reading years later. The strong relation of the "analysis of phoneme position test" to the children's success in reading at the end of the project certainly suggests that awareness of phonemes also plays a part, but we have to be a bit careful here. In some of the trials of this apparently rather difficult test the children had to recognise the opening sound of the word and therefore its onset. The trouble is that Lundberg and his colleagues only related the total score for this test to reading later on. We need to know whether it was just the children's ability to recognise onsets that predicted their reading or whether their awareness of phonemes in other parts of the word also played a part in predicting the children's reading.

We have one other criticism of this study. It does not satisfy our requirement for specificity. The only "outcome measures", as they are often called, were the children's reading and spelling. It is just possible (though it seems to us highly unlikely) that the phonological scores would have predicted all manner of educational skills (mathematics, counting) as well as reading. We do need to know whether phonological skills are related just to reading.

2. Rhyming and Reading: The First Oxford Project

We have remarked already on the near impossibility of finding a decent measure of phoneme detection in children who are still too young to go to school. This is a problem for psychologists in Britain where children go to school at five years and for American psychologists where the age for starting school is six years. It is also a problem which Lundberg and his colleagues were able to avoid by being Swedish, for in that happy country children do not go to school until they are seven years old. So it is much easier for psychologists who carry out longitudinal studies about the causes of reading and who do not live in Scandinavian countries to turn instead to phonological skills which children obviously do possess before they go to school.

Rhyme and alliteration are the obvious solution. Children can recognise rhyme and alliteration long before they begin to read, as we have seen, and the fact that they do so shows that they can categorise words by their onsets and their rimes. There are grounds too (Chapter 4) for thinking that these speech units play an important part in children's reading: children understand that certain letter sequences signify particular onsets and rimes. All this suggests that children's early rhyming skills play an important part in their eventual success in reading, and so we have an idea that can be readily tested in a longitudinal study.

If this idea is right there should be a strong and specific relationship between measures of sensitivity to rhyme taken some time before children begin to read and their success in reading years later. If this relationship does not exist many of the claims that we made in the first five chapters of this book would be quite wrong.

Lundberg's work which we have just described showed beyond doubt that children's ability to rhyme is a strong and valuable predictor of reading, but in that study the measures of rhyme were given to children who were rather old at the time: they were at an age when in England or America they would already have been schoolchildren. We need to know whether tests of rhyme given to children much younger than this—children of three or four years—also predict reading and spelling.

Bradley and Bryant (1983, 1985) set up a large-scale longitudinal study of the relationship between children's sensitivity to rhyme before they read and their success in reading later on. Their reason for wanting to do this study went back to their discovery (Bradley & Bryant, 1978) that backward readers are often far worse than other children (even in a reading level match experiment) at detecting and also at producing rhyme. This result suggested a causal hypothesis. Rhyme may play a widespread role in every child's reading. The more sensitive a child is to rhyme the quicker she will learn to read: the more insensitive, the more difficulties she will have with reading.

But this idea was only suggested, and certainly was not proved, by the 1978 study of backward readers. One cannot be certain that a factor (in this case rhyme) which affects backward readers has the same effect on other children too. Backward readers may read in quite idiosyncratic ways. We needed another study to show whether the connection between rhyme and reading applies to children at large.

Bradley and Bryant worked with a large group children (they were 403 in number at the beginning of the project and had dwindled to 368 at the end) who were either four or five years old when the project began and either eight or nine years when they were seen for the last time three to four years later. None of the children could read when they were seen for the first time (those who showed any sign of being able to read were not included in the project), and all of them had made some progress with reading and with spelling by the end of the project.

When the experimenters first saw each child they gave him or her the rhyme and alliteration oddity tests which we mentioned in Chapters 1 and 4. In these the experimenter read out three or four words at a time. All but one of the words had a sound in common, and the child had to judge which word was the odd one out (e.g. "sit" in the set "pin", "win", "sit", "fin"). At the same time the child was given a vocabulary test, and a memory test as well. The reason for this last test was that the judgements that she had to make in the oddity test depended on her being able to remember the three or four words read out to her, and so the experimenters needed a measure of the child's ability to recall these words.

Three years or more later at the end of the project the children were given standardised tests of reading and of spelling, and also an I.Q. test. They were also given a standardised test of mathematical skills.

Bradley and Bryant found that there was a strong and also a specific relationship between the children's initial sensitivity to rhyme and alliteration and the progress that they made in learning to read and to spell over the following three years. This relationship held even after controls for the effects of differences in I.Q., in their vocabulary and also in their initial memory scores had been included. Furthermore, the relationship turned out to be a specific one. The children's rhyming scores always predicted their success in reading and spelling and never predicted their arithmetical skills. It was the same with the alliteration scores of the children who were four at the beginning of the project. The one exception was the alliteration test that was given to the children who were five years old when the project started. Their scores in this test predicted their arithmetical skills at the end of the project as well their reading and spelling scores. This means that in some cases the alliteration test may tap rather broad educational skills. The relation between rhyme and reading and spelling, however, is remarkably specific.

So the project establishes the answer to one question but it raises another. Is there a connection between children's sensitivity to rhyme and their awareness of phonemes? If such a connection exists, is it direct or does it work indirectly through children's experiences of reading?

3. Phoneme Detection and Rhyme: The Second Oxford Project.

It is time we took stock of what we know. These are some of the facts.

Children can recognise rhyme and alliteration long before they go to school, and there is a connection between their ability to do so and their success in reading later on. On the other hand, young children have great difficulty with tasks in which they have to isolate and manipulate phonemes and on the whole only begin to be able to cope with tasks of this sort either when they start to read or even some time after that.

So the developmental sequence seems to take this form. First, children are aware of rhyme. Then later on they are taught to read and write. At roughly the same time as they begin reading they start to isolate phonemes, and their ability to do so grows markedly in the next few years.

What are the connections between these events? As far as we can see, people have worked with three possible theoretical models, and we present these in Fig. 6.1.

We owe Model 1 to the Belgian group whose work we described in the first chapter (Morais, Alegria & Content, 1987). They argue that children become aware of phonemes as a direct result of learning how to use the alphabet, and they also claim that awareness of rhyme involves phonological units that are too global to have much effect on children's reading. So in this model there is no link between rhyme and children's reading, and the children's awareness of phonemes is a product of reading.

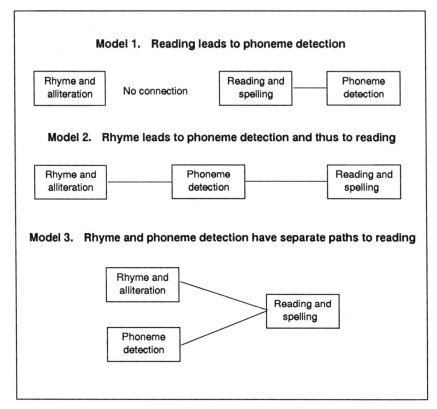

Model 1.   Reading leads to phoneme detection

| Rhyme and alliteration | No connection | | Reading and spelling |————| Phoneme detection |

Model 2.   Rhyme leads to phoneme detection and thus to reading

| Rhyme and alliteration |————| Phoneme detection |————| Reading and spelling |

Model 3.   Rhyme and phoneme detection have separate paths to reading

FIG. 6.1.   Three models of the relationship between reading and phonological awareness.

The model certainly provides an explanation for the development of phoneme detection, and it is an explanation for which there is a great deal of evidence (which we described in earlier chapters). But the model must be wrong in one respect. The data produced by Lundberg and his colleagues, and by Bradley and Bryant, establish a strong connection between children's sensitivity to rhyme before they read and their reading some time later. Yet Model 1 insists that there is no connection. So the model is, at best, incomplete. This model, it should be noted, predicts no relation between rhyme and phoneme detection.

In Model 2 there is a direct connection between rhyme and phoneme detection, and only an indirect connection between rhyme and reading. According to this model children start by being aware of the relatively gross phonological units involved in rhyme and alliteration, but this phonological awareness becomes more and more refined until finally they can detect the much smaller unit of the phoneme. This allows them to learn about grapheme-phoneme correspondences and thus helps them to read.

This model predicts a strong relationship between children's scores in rhyme tasks when they are, say, three or four years old and their success in phoneme detection tasks when they are five or six. It also predicts that these early rhyme scores will be related to reading, but only indirectly because rhyme leads to phoneme detection which in turn affects reading. So the relationship between rhyme and reading should disappear if the controls are made for differences in the children's ability to detect phonemes.

Model 3 is similar to the theory that we have been pursuing throughout this book. According to this model there is a direct connection between rhyme and reading, and this connection is quite independent of the relation between awareness of phonemes and reading. Rhyme makes a contribution because it allows children to connect sequences of letters with onsets and rimes. Awareness of phonemes has an effect because it leads to the formation of grapheme-phoneme relations. The model leads to one main prediction: it is that the relationship between children's awareness of rhyme and reading will hold even after controls for differences in the children's ability to detect phonemes.

These models were tested in a second longitudinal study (Bryant et al., in press). This was quite different in form from the first. Fewer children were involved—64 in all—and they were given many more tests and seen much more often than the children in the earlier project.

The study lasted for three years, from the time the children were three and a quarter until they were just over six and a half years old. The children were given tests of rhyme and alliteration at different points in the project, and one interesting result was that most of the children were able to do quite well in a rhyme oddity task even at the age of three and a quarter. Predictably, the phoneme detection tasks were a great deal harder, and it was only possible to measure their ability to break words into phonemes after they were five years old. The tests of phoneme detection were versions of the Liberman et al. (1974) phoneme tapping task, and of the Content et al. (1982) phoneme deletion task. At the end of the project, the experimenters measured the children's reading and spelling skills, and also (for the reasons given above) they gave the children an arithmetic test as well.

Once again, the rhyme scores predicted the children's progress in reading over the following years extremely well, even after controls for differences in the children's intelligence, their vocabulary and their social background were included; and once again the relationship was specific: rhyme predicted reading but not the children's mathematical skills.

Both the phoneme detection measures also predicted the children's reading but not as well as the rhyme scores did, and the phoneme deletion measure also passed the specificity test; it predicted reading but not arithmetic. However, the phoneme tapping test was as strongly related to the children's scores in the arithmetic test as their reading scores, and therefore we cannot claim a specific connection between phoneme tapping and reading. It seems likely that the strong connection between that test and arithmetic is due to the fact that in the tapping task children do not just break words into phonemes, they also have to count how many phonemes there are in each of the words.

We come now to the two crucial questions: do rhyme scores predict children's ability to detect phonemes? Also, do these rhyme scores predict reading and spelling even after controls for differences in the children's ability to detect phonemes? Model 1 suggests a negative answer to both questions. Model 2 produces a positive answer to the first question, but a negative answer to the second. Model 3 suggests a negative answer to the first question, and a positive one to the second.

The answers to both questions were positive. The children's rhyme scores were strongly related to their success in the phoneme detection tasks some time later, even after the usual controls for extraneous differences. That result fits well with Model 2. But it was also the case that these same rhyme scores predicted the children's success in reading even after the effects of differences in the children's ability to detect phonemes (as well as the effect of the other extraneous variables) had been controlled. We can therefore be quite sure that there is a direct link between rhyme and reading, as Model 3 suggests. Rhyme makes an independent and distinctive contribution to reading.

It seems that a combination of Models 2 and 3 gives us the most convincing account of children's phonological development and its relationship to their reading. Spelling, on the other hand, is a completely different matter.

Model 2 accounts for the relationships that were found between rhyme scores, phoneme detection scores and spelling perfectly well. The children's rhyme scores predicted their performance in the spelling test, but this relation disappeared when controls were made for differences in the children's ability to detect phonemes, exactly as Model 2 predicts. Rhyme does not make a direct or independent contribution to children's spelling.

Further Evidence on the New Model

The new model (the combination of Models 2 and 3) provides a framework to help us assess other longitudinal studies. We can see whether they confirm our claim that children's rhyming skills and their ability to detect phonemes make separate contributions to children's reading.

One study which fits well with the model is a three-year longitudinal study by Ellis and Large (1987). The experimenters saw the children first when they were five years old and then tested them again at yearly intervals until they were eight years old. Each time that they saw the children, Ellis and Large gave them several phonological tasks, which included the Bradley and Bryant oddity tasks, sound blending, and phoneme and syllable segmentation. They also tested the children's memory.

When the children were eight years old, the experimenters selected three groups of five children from the main group. One group had a high I.Q. but a low reading level (group A), another had a high I.Q. and good reading level (group B), and the third a low I.Q. and a poor reading level (group C). The authors then looked back at the way that the children in these three groups had managed the various tests during the preceding three years. They wanted to know which of their tests were the best predictors of who would fall into each of these three groups.

The best predictors were the rhyme tests. The original scores of groups A and B on the rhyme test were very different. The children in group A who were to become poor readers despite their good I.Q.s did very poorly on the rhyme oddity test and fairly badly on the test of rhyme production as well. The other group of poor readers (group C) had also not managed to cope at all well with the rhyme oddity task. So Ellis and Large's data support the claim that rhyme makes a distinctive contribution to reading.

Scrambled Data

Some studies include measures of children's rhyming skills and of their capacity to detect phonemes, and yet lump these scores together as though they represent one variable. This is a pity, since the two kinds of measure in our view are, if not as different from each other as chalk from cheese, as different as, say, Brie from Caerphilly. We shall mention these lost opportunities briefly.

One is a massive project by Share, Jorm, MacLean and Matthews (1984). They studied a group of 543 children for a period of three years. The children were five at the start of the study, and were seen again when they were six and seven years old. At the beginning of the study the experimenters gave the children a segmentation test (as well as a very large number of other linguistic tests). The children were asked to divide one syllable words either into the first sound and the rest of the word (c-at) or into its beginning, middle and end sounds (c-a-t). From the point of view of our model the difference between these two conditions is extremely interesting, as the first involves a division between onset and rime and the second between phonemes. But the authors of the study treated the two tasks as one task. They put them together to form one "phonological segmentation" score.

In fact, this score turned out to be the strongest predictor of children's reading skills over the following two years. Share and his colleagues report that it predicted reading much better even than the children's initial vocabulary scores. But they made no attempt to separate the two components of this strikingly successful test.

We encounter the same failure to take proper advantage of some interesting data in another longitudinal study by Stuart and M. Coltheart (1988). This was a project that lasted for four years. The authors first saw the children—only 23 in number—when they were four and a half years old. At that time they gave the children several phoneme detection tasks, two rhyme tasks and a syllable task as well. Then they monitored the progress that the children made in reading over the next four years. Stuart and Coltheart report a relation between the children's "phonological score" and their reading age at the time when they first tested the children's reading at five and a half years, and subsequently whenever they tested the children's reading up to the age of eight years.

There are several reasons for caution about this claim, but the most serious, we think, is that the "phonological score" is simply an amalgam of all the phonological tests—phonemes, rhymes and syllables. Here again an opportunity to look at the relationships between some very different phonological skills and the development of reading has been lost.

There is another problem too. We cannot be sure that the relation between the children's phonological scores and their subsequent progress in reading is a genuine one. Though the authors did measure the children's I.Q. and did do multiple regressions, they did not manage to control for differences in the children's I.Q. effectively. They should have entered the children's I.Q. as the first step in the multiple regression, in the way that we set out earlier in this chapter, but they did not.

Wimmer (in press) has pointed out another reason for doubting the relation that Stuart and Coltheart report between the phonological scores and reading. He notes that there was actually no relation between the children's pre-school phonological score and the first measure that the experimenters took of their reading. The relation only became significant when Stuart and Coltheart combined the phonological scores with another, later measure—a measure of letter-sound knowledge which they took at the same time as they measured the children's reading. This makes Stuart and Coltheart's claim of a connection between children's phonological skills and their early reading a highly questionable one.

Studies which Appear to Contradict our Model

At the beginning of this chapter we raised the problem of the unknown *tertium quid* the possibility that a correlation might give the impression of a connection which does not exist. The two variables may correlate because both are determined by some other unknown factor. Bowey and Patel (1988) have suggested that the connection between rhyme and reading may be a spurious one for this reason. They base their claim on a correlational study (not a longitudinal one) of 60 six year old children, whose reading they tested and to whom they gave the Bradley and Bryant rhyme oddity test. (They wrongly called this a test of "phonemic awareness". This is the sort of misnomer that gives rhyme a bad name: rhyme involves awareness of rimes, not of phonemes.) They also gave two other linguistic tests. One was a "sentence imitation" task in which the children simply had to repeat a set of sentences of varying complexity, and the other was a vocabulary test.

Bowey and Patel found the usual relationship between rhyme and reading even after they had controlled for the effects of differences in the children's vocabulary. But they also found that this relationship disappeared if they controlled for differences in the children's scores in the other two linguistic tests. On the other hand there was a significant connection between the children's scores in these two tests and their reading skills even after controls for differences in the rhyme task.

The authors concluded that the important factor is children's "general language ability". This determines reading, according to them, and affects children's awareness of sounds as well. However, we find it hard to accept this conclusion, because we think that it can be shown that Bowey and Patel measured rhyme too late.

The second Oxford longitudinal study which we began to describe earlier also included linguistic tests which were very similar to the ones administered by Bowey and Patel. The data (Bryant, MacLean & Bradley, in press) show quite clearly that the children's scores in rhyme oddity tests which were given to them when they were four years old were strongly related to their reading levels at six years of age even after controls for differences in the syntactic awareness task. The children's pre-school experience with rhyme makes an independent contribution to reading.

Another claim has been made that does not fit well with our model. The claim is that longitudinal studies show that phonological awareness affects children's reading only because it influences their ability to learn grapheme-phoneme correspondences. Tunmer and Nesdale (1985) produced this idea in the study that we described earlier in this chapter, and Tunmer, Herriman and Nesdale (1988) have reiterated it on the basis of very similar evidence in a later longitudinal study. In both studies the children's scores in a phoneme tapping task did not predict their reading levels later on if differences in the children's ability to read nonsense words were taken into account. (These experimenters used a statistical technique called path analysis which is based on multiple regression.) The experimenters assumed that children have to use grapheme-phoneme correspondences in order to read nonsense words, and therefore concluded that the pattern of results which we have just described meant that children's phonological awareness influences their ability to learn about the relations between graphemes and phonemes which in turn affects their reading. That they claimed is the only pathway: phonological awareness makes no other contribution to reading.

The result is an interesting one, and the authors' conclusions are different from ours. But their conclusion is based on studies which involved one phonological test only, and that a phoneme detection test. In fact we agree with Tunmer and his colleagues that children's awareness of phonemes is connected to reading because children learn to use grapheme-phoneme correspondences. But the evidence that we have reviewed shows that rhyme affects reading in an entirely different way. There would, we predict, be quite a different pattern of results if the children were given a rhyme test as well as a phoneme test. If rhyme makes a contribution to reading which has nothing to do with grapheme-phoneme correspondences, as we have suggested, the relationship between rhyme and reading would still hold even after differences in the children's performance in the nonsense word task had been controlled.

Our conclusion about the work that we have discussed in this chapter can be summarised in two sentences. Tests of children's awareness of rhyme and alliteration (rime and onset) predict reading (but usually not mathematics) even after controls for differences in intelligence and social background. These tests pass what we called the minimum requirement for a causal variable: children's awareness of rhyme may well influence their progress in reading and may also play a role in other forms of phonological development, such as the growth of sensitivity to phonemes.

CHAPTER 7

Teaching Children about Sounds

THE NEED FOR "TRAINING STUDIES"

Children are taught to read. They have to be taught about the alphabet and they have to be shown how to use it because the whole system of linking words and sounds to written symbols is an arbitrary one. Of course, teaching is not everything. As we have seen children make their own considerable contribution: they "invent" spelling with great ingenuity and they make inferences about the spelling patterns of quite unfamiliar words. Nevertheless, teaching is clearly an important part of learning to read.

So any discovery about skills which children depend on in order to learn to read is directly relevant to the question of teaching. If we know what skills are needed we can help children by seeing to it that they have those skills. Our argument, that certain phonological skills play a crucial role in children's reading, is as good an example as any. If we are right, parents and teachers should try to make sure that their children have a feel for phonemes, onsets and rimes, and realise how important they are in written language.

But this is nothing more than a thoroughly trite statement. Teachers have for centuries been showing children how letters signify sounds and how collections of letters represent collections of sounds which add up to meaningful words. Of course, there has been a great deal of debate about the value of the "phonic" approach. But many teachers agree that children need to be taught about the relationships between letters and sounds, and ought to be shown how to blend sounds into words and how to break words into sounds, when they start to learn to read and write. So what is new?

If our argument suggests something new, it is that parents and teachers should put as much emphasis on the connection between the onset and rime units and sequences of letters ("str-ing") as they do on the relation between phonemes and single letters

117

("c-a-t"). But we hesitate even here, for we have not yet produced any evidence on the consequences of teaching children to attend to sounds.

We can be certain of one thing. This kind of teaching should help children to learn to read, if there is anything to the argument that we have been developing in this book. In fact, studies in which children are taught about sounds give us the best chance to test the idea of a causal connection directly. Training experiments are causal experiments. If you teach phonological skills to a group of children and their reading improves as a direct result of this teaching, you will have shown that these children's awareness of sounds did affect their reading.

So there are two quite distinct roles for training experiments. One is educational: these experiments can tell us about effective (and ineffective) ways of teaching children to read. The other is to test hypotheses about the causal connection between children's phonological awareness and the way that they learn to read. There is, in fact, a certain tension between these two roles, because they lead to very different kinds of project. Educational studies which establish perfectly well that a particular educational method works are usually quite inadequate tests of ideas about a specific causal connection between phonological skills and reading. And experiments designed to test this specific hypothesis rarely produce worthwhile suggestions about educational methods. These are two different genres. We can see why by looking first at some educational studies.

EDUCATIONAL STUDIES OF THE PHONOLOGICAL CONNECTION

In real life—in real classrooms—children are not taught just about sounds. "Phonic" methods involve teaching children about sounds and about their relation to alphabetic letters and written words. So when people study the effectiveness of these methods, they naturally teach the children about the alphabet as well as about sounds—about graphemes as well as about phonemes. There is no harm in this. In fact it has to be done if the study is to reflect "real" teaching. Studies of this sort can demonstrate that this or that teaching method works, but they do not establish a causal connection between children's phonological awareness and the way that they learn to read.

The trouble is this: if the children are taught about alphabetic letters as well as about sounds, we cannot be certain that training about sounds *per se* has helped them to read. The study does not definitely show a causal link between phonological awareness and reading, because it might have been the experience that the children had with alphabetic letters that caused the improvement in reading. That improvement, therefore, may have had nothing directly to do with the phonological training. Of course, any successful demonstration that phonic teaching methods work is of great interest to anyone interested in the phonological hypothesis, but it does not establish that the hypothesis is definitely right. But we can at least say that demonstrations that children benefit from phonic methods do add to the plausibility of this hypothesis, and might give us hints about how to test it in other projects. That is our reason for describing two of the most interesting attempts to establish the value of phonic teaching methods.

One of the first, and still one of the most important, attempts to show that children read better after being taught about phonemes was described by M.A. Wallach and L. Wallach in a book that they produced in 1976. Their project lasted for 30 weeks, and while it lasted they taught, in daily half-hour sessions, a group of seven year old children about the sounds of the alphabet, about the initial sounds in words, oral segmentation of words into initial sound and rime (as in "b-ird") and then into constituent sounds ("b-e-d"), and oral blending training ("m-a-n" to "man"). Later on they also taught the children about the connection between written and spoken sounds and words. Wallach and Wallach also formed a control group of children of the same age, but this was an "unseen" control group. They received no training and no extra attention during those 30 weeks.

After the training the experimenters gave all the children in the project various reading tasks: the children had to read lists of single words, and some prose as well. Both groups were given a test of reading. The children who had been given the extra training in phonological awareness turned out to be a great deal better at reading than the children in the control group. In contrast, there was no difference between the groups in mathematical skills.

So here is a successful educational study which provides strong support for the idea that phonic training helps in learning to read. It also fits well with the hypothesis that children's phonological skills influence the progress that they make in reading. But, for reasons that we have already given, it is not a strong test of that hypothesis. The experimenters used written material during the training and they had a perfectly good reason for doing so, which was that they were looking at the effectiveness of a particular method of teaching which worked that way. But as a result we cannot be certain that the phonological teaching *per se* did affect the children's reading.

It is a similar story with the next highly successful educational study that we shall describe. Joanna Williams (1980) worked with children between the ages of seven and 12, most of whom had relatively low I.Q.s; their mean I.Q. was 83. Her project lasted for 18 weeks. She divided the children into an experimental and a control group and gave lessons in phonological training to the children in the first of these groups: she began by teaching them to break words into syllables and later into phonemes, and went on to teach them to blend phonemes into words. Following this, she taught them about letter-sound relationships: these children "received extensive practice in the manipulation of these letters so that he/she could decode (read) and construct from letter squares (spell) all the possible CVC combinations" (p. 3). The children in the control group were not given any training or extra attention at all.

At the end of the project Williams gave the children real words and nonsense words to read, and she too reported that the children in the experimental group read significantly more words and nonsense words than those in the control group. It is a heartening result, and we can be pleased at the fact that Williams has found a way to help children who are obviously at some disadvantage at school. But again, although the results fit well with the phonological hypothesis, we cannot be certain that the children's reading improved because of the extra phonological experiences that they were given. These children were also taught about the alphabet.

Thus these two respectable and highly successful educational studies lend credence to the idea that children's phonological skills are involved in their reading, but they do not test the hypothesis directly enough for us to be sure of the causal connection. We are forced to turn to more academic and less realistic experiments for evidence for that specific connection.

Training Experiments that test the Phonological Hypothesis Directly

Training studies that test the phonological connection, by much the same token, are usually quite inadequate evidence as far as teaching methods are concerned. To test the connection you have to look at the effect of teaching sounds on its own and that, as we have remarked, is not the phonic method. So the training studies that we are about to review are to some extent quite artificial, but they do produce extremely useful information.

Such experiments can test the general hypothesis that a child's awareness of sounds affects his or her reading, and they can do a great deal more as well. We are at the stage when we want the answer to quite specific questions about the effects of phonological awareness. We want to know, for example, whether children's awareness of onset and rime has one sort of effect, and their sensitivity to phonemes quite a different effect, on their reading. In principle, there is no reason at all why specific questions like this cannot be answered in training experiments, and in fact some extremely interesting work on different ways of teaching children about sounds does solve some of the problems about causal connections.

The questions that we want answered are simple and obvious. Are children who are learning to read helped by being taught to be aware of phonemes? Is it a help to them to have been taught about onset and rime—about alliteration and rhyme? And do these two kinds of teaching have different effects on reading? Some of the studies that we shall describe involve both kinds of teaching, and others one but not the other.

Before we start, we should like to mention that we are limiting our account of research on training to a relatively small number of studies. Some time ago we wrote a review (Bryant & Goswami, 1987) of training studies, and we concluded that many of them were not relevant to the question of a possible causal connection between phonological skills and reading. One of the main reasons was that in many of the experiments the outcome measure was not a test of reading but a task which was an analogue of reading. This took the form of reading nonsense words or learning some artificial sound-symbol associations. For the sake of simplicity we have decided not to write about these experiments here.

TEACHING CHILDREN ABOUT BOTH
PHONEMES, AND ONSET AND RIME

There can be little doubt now that training in phonological awareness usually helps children to read. One of the reasons for being sure that this is so is to be found in the results of an extremely interesting study by Cunningham (1988). The training that she gave to the children in her project was in awareness of onset and rime, and of phonemes as well. But her main interest was in the idea that children need to be "conceptually aware" of the reasons for the importance of phonological skills. The children whom she worked with were six and seven year olds, and they were divided into three groups: a "conceptual" group, who received phonological training (of which more later) and were also given conceptual lessons on the links between phonological awareness and reading; a "skill and drill" group, who received the phonological training alone; and a control group, who spent the same amount of time as the experimental groups reading and discussing stories with their teacher but who were given no phonological training.

The training given to the children in the two experimental groups involved concentrated experience of segmentation and of blending the sounds in real and nonsense words. The project lasted for 10 weeks. It began with the children breaking words into onset and rime and continued later with them doing the same thing with phonemes.

Cunningham looked at two outcomes. She wanted to know whether she really had improved the phonological skills of the two experimental groups, and so she gave them tests of phonological awareness before the training started and after it was finished. These tests were: a version of the phoneme deletion test developed by Bruce (1964), the Lindamood Auditory Conceptualisation Test which we described in Chapter 6, and the oddity rhyme task devised by Bradley and Bryant (1983). Cunningham reports that the children in the two experimental groups were much better in the post-tests of phonological skills than in the pre-tests, and that their improvement was markedly greater than that of the children in the control group. So she had managed to teach the skills that she set out to teach.

The other question was about the effects on reading. Again Cunningham found a greater improvement in the two experimental groups than in the control group. She also reports that among the younger children the "conceptual" group made more progress in reading than the children in the other experimental group. This is an interesting result, but we will concentrate on the fact that phonological training did improve the children's reading. Cunningham's results establish a general pattern, but do not answer our specific question. The phonological training helped children to read, but that training was about onset and rime and about phonemes too. Do both kinds of training have an effect?

The results of another study which also involved teaching both about rime (rhyme) and about phonemes provide the beginnings of an answer to this question. This was a large-scale training study which was carried out in Denmark by Lundberg, Frost and Petersen (1988). They worked with six year old children, who were not yet at school.

(In Denmark children first go to school when they are seven.) These children lived in two quite separate geographical areas. The children from one area formed the experimental group which was taught to be more aware of sounds. The control group consisted of the children who lived in another part of the country: these children were given no extra training at all (Fig.7.1).

Let us look at the phonological training given to the experimental group. It consisted of a series of games and exercises which the children were given every day. The training programme began with easy listening games (verbal and non-verbal sounds). Later on in the study the children were given some rhyming exercises (nursery rhymes, rhymed stories and games for rhyme production), and after that they began to be taught to break

Pre-tests (6 years)	Post-tests (7 years)	School measures (Grades 1 and 2)
Standardised tests		
Pre-reading skill	Pre-reading skill	
Letter knowledge	Letter knowledge	
Language comprehension	Language comprehension	
Vocabulary	Vocabulary	
Phonological awareness		*Grade 1*
Rhyme	Rhyme	Rhyme
Word segmentation	Word segmentation	
Syllable synthesis	Syllable synthesis	
Syllable segmentation	Syllable segmentation	Syllable segmentation
Initial phoneme	Initial phoneme	Initial phoneme
Phoneme segmentation	Phoneme segmentation	Phoneme segmentation
Phoneme synthesis	Phoneme synthesis	
		Word length
		Raven's I.Q.
		Mathematics
		Reading
		Spelling
		Grade 2
		Reading
		Spelling

FIG. 7.1.   Design of the Swedish training study (Lundberg et al., 1988).

up sentences into words. Then they learned to break words into syllables, and by the second month of the project, into phonemes as well. During the project the children were taught nothing directly about reading.

Lundberg and his colleagues were interested in two possible outcomes of the training and the relations between them. They wanted to know how the training affected the children's awareness of sounds and also what effects the training had on their reading. Just before the training began and just after it finished the experimenters gave the children various tests of linguistic awareness which were measures of their ability to detect words, syllables, phonemes and also rhyme. During the following year when the children were seven years old and had been at school for seven months, Lundberg and his colleagues gave them reading and spelling tests and tests of mathematics, and a year later still tested their reading and spelling once again.

The immediate aim of the project was fulfilled. The phonological training had an effect on the children's phonological skills. Before training, the children in the control group were rather better than those in the experimental group in tasks in which they had to detect phonemes: by the end of the eight-month training the scores of the experimental group in these tasks far outstripped those of the control children. It was different with rhyme. The two groups did as well as each other in the rhyme test given to them at the start of the training, and when this training finished the children in the experimental group were better than the children in the other group, but only slightly better. The different effects on the two kinds of measure is extremely interesting from the point of view of the hypothesis that we have outlined in previous chapters, as we have argued that the detection of phonemes and the detection of rhyme are to some extent independent activities. But we think that some caution is needed about the experimenters' conclusion that the training had little effect on the children's rhyming skills. It is clear from the figures given by Lundberg and his colleagues that the children in both groups were near "ceiling" in the rhyme post-test. The children in both groups made very few mistakes in that post-test which, therefore, was too easy. It would not detect a difference between the two groups if one existed.

The training also had a considerable effect on the children's reading and spelling. Those who were given the training could read and spell more words than the children in the control group, and the effect seems to have been specific. In the mathematics test the scores of the experimental group were actually lower than the other group's. This is evidence that training in sounds does help children to read more effectively. But the study shows more than just that. The fact that the main phonological effect of the training was an improvement in the children's ability to detect phonemes implies that the improvement in the children's reading was a direct result of their increased sensitivity to phonemes.

So children's awareness of phonemes plays a part. What about rhyme? The fact that the training may not have improved the children's rhyming skills in this study suggests that rhyme played no part in the improvement in these children's reading. But this does not mean that rhyme is unimportant in reading. That would only be shown by a study in which the children's rhyming skills improved, but their reading did not. The question of the importance of rhyme in children's reading is left entirely open by this study.

Teaching Children about Onset and Rime

We shall now describe two studies that support the idea that teaching children to attend to onset and rime does help them to learn to read and spell words. The first of these was an experiment on the importance of rhyme (Bradley & Bryant, 1983, 1985). This was a study with two parts. One part, which we described in Chapter 6, consisted of longitudinal data on a large number of children. The other part, which involved a smaller number—65 children—was a training study. These children were six years old when the training started. All of them had been given the Bradley and Bryant rhyme oddity test when they were four or five years old and had done rather poorly in it.

The children were divided into two experimental and two control groups. One of the experimental groups was given training in rhyme and alliteration over a period of two years, while they were six and seven years old. The children in the second experimental group were also taught about rhyme and alliteration during the same period, but in the second year they were taught as well to represent the sounds of the words with alphabetic letters. The children in one of the control groups were also taught for the same amount of time to put words (the same words) into categories, but these were conceptual categories (animate vs. inanimate, indoor objects vs. outdoor objects). The experimenters gave the children in the other control group no added experience.

When these children were eight years old they were given standardised tests of reading, spelling and mathematics. The hypothesis that children's rhyming skills affect their reading produces the prediction that the first of the experimental groups (trained just to categorise words by rhyme and alliteration) should be better at reading and spelling than the first of the control groups (trained just to categorise words by conceptual categories). This was what happened: there was a consistent three- to four-month difference between the two groups in their reading and spelling ages. However, there was also a lot of variation within the two groups, and as a result the difference between them fell just short of statistical significance. So we have evidence here that rhyme does affect reading and spelling, but the evidence is not as strong as we should like it to be (Fig.7.2).

Another result is worth mentioning. The children in the group taught about letters as well as about rhyme did far better than any of the other groups in reading and spelling (although not in mathematics). In many ways this result fits better with the educational studies that we have described because it involved training about the alphabet as well as training about sound. The result tells us of a powerful teaching method but does not on its own establish a connection between children's awareness of sounds and their reading.

The second direct study on the effects of training children about onset and rime was done by Wise, Olson and Treiman (1990). They wanted to know whether children learn to read words particularly easily if these words are explicitly divided into onset and rime units. The experimenters' technique was to present written words on a computer

	Experimental groups		Control groups	
	I Phonological categorisation	**II** Plastic letters	**III** Conceptual categorisation	**IV** Unseen
Reading (Schonell)	92.23	96.96	88.48	84.46
Reading (Neale)	93.47	99.77	89.09	85.70
Spelling (Schonell)	85.97	98.81	81.76	75.15
Maths	91.27	91.09	87.99	84.13

FIG. 7.2.   Results of the Oxford training study (Bradley & Bryant, 1983). Final reading, spelling and mathematics levels (months) adjusted for age and I.Q.

monitor, and to highlight the first part and then the second part of each word separately. At the same time a speech synthesiser produced the sound that was associated with the part of the word being highlighted. The point of the experiment was that sometimes the words were separated at the onset-rime border (f/ork, sl/ip) and sometimes not (ju/nk, co/rn).

Wise, Olson and Treiman measured how well the children learned in the two conditions by giving them the same words to read after the training had finished, and then once again later in the session. As they expected the children were better at reading the words which had been separated at the onset-rime boundary than those which had not. Wise and her colleagues concluded, and it seems a reasonable conclusion, that the onset-rime boundary is an important one for children learning to read, and therefore that the children's awareness of onset and rime plays a part in their reading.

The experiment, it should be noted, is a limited one. Each child was seen in one session only, and we do not know how long after that session they were able to go on reading these words. We do not even know exactly what caused the effect. Would there have been the same results if the spelling sequences had not been highlighted, and the children had simply heard the word divided into onset and rime? Nevertheless, this is a very good start. Training experiments do support the idea that onset and rime play a crucial role in children's reading.

CHAPTER 8

Do Children Learn to Read (and Fail to Learn to Read) in Different Ways from each Other?

There are several ways to read (and to spell) a word. One can decipher it letter by letter: one can divide the word into letter sequences and relate each sequence (-"ing", -"ight") to a sound; one can recognise the word as a distinctive visual pattern: one can remember that whole sequences of letters signify a particular word ("l" "a" "u" "g" "h" means "laugh"). What significance does this abundant choice of strategies have for children who are trying to learn to read?

Up to this point our answer to this question has been entirely developmental. By "developmental answer" we mean the idea that all children progress in the same way, acquiring the same skills in the same order when they learn to read and spell. For example, we have claimed that when children begin to read they tend to recognise words as wholes and only analyse them phonologically some time later on. (We will be discussing our developmental model of reading and spelling, and other people's models, in some detail in the next chapter.)

However, there is another possible consequence of the choice that children have of different reading strategies. It is that there are differences between children which are not developmental. Some children may rely on one strategy, and some on quite another. There are people who argue that the main effect of the abundance of different ways to read is that individual children soon adopt a distinctive style of reading, and that different children take to different styles. In many ways this idea is the antithesis of the notion that there is a normal course of development in reading which all children go through. According to theories about normal development, as we shall see in more detail in Chapter 9, the strategy that a child uses to read depends entirely on the stage of reading that she happens to be at. But theories about individual differences hold that two children who are at the same stage in reading may nevertheless adopt quite different strategies from each other: the particular way that they read is a result of psychological differences between them and has little to do with their stage of reading.

So before we set out our ideas about the typical development of reading in the final chapter, we must ask first whether there are many different ways to learn to read.

DIFFERENCES AMONG NORMAL READERS

Normal Readers

In the 1970s and in much of the 1980s most theoretical accounts of reading were dominated by the idea of there being "two routes" to reading. One was the "visual" route and the other the "phonological" route (Marshall & Newcombe, 1973; M. Coltheart, 1978). When people wrote about the phonological route they made it clear, on the whole, that they were thinking of grapheme-phoneme correspondences. We disagree with this two-way split, mainly because we think that there are two distinct phonological codes, one which deals with onset and rime and the other with phonemes (see also Patterson & Morton, 1985). We mention the old-style two-route model now because of its effect on the ideas people had about individual differences at the time.

An example is the hypothesis about individual differences which was originally put forward by Baron and developed by Baron and Treiman. They claimed that you can divide people who read English into "Phoenicians" and "Chinese". Phoenicians are those who depend most heavily on a phonological code when they read and write. Chinese readers on the other hand depend largely on visual memory: they recognise words as patterns and remember them as patterns when they have to write. The reason for these striking labels is fairly obvious. The alphabet, and thus the whole idea of grapheme-phoneme correspondences, was invented by the Phoenicians (Gelb, 1963), and therefore people who depend on these correspondences are called after them. Chinese people, on the other hand, read a logographic script, which means that they have to read words as patterns, and that is why Baron decided to give this label to people who read English words as wholes.

So Baron and Treiman accepted the two-route idea, but added the claim that some people rely more on one route and some more on the other. Their evidence that people can be classified in this way involves the most ingenious use of correlations.

Baron (1979), in a study which we mentioned in Chapter 4, started by giving children aged nine years three lists of words to read. These were: regular words ("cut"), which can be deciphered letter by letter through letter-sound relationships, irregular words ("put"), which cannot be read in such a way, and nonsense words ("lut"), which he assumed could only be read by grapheme-phoneme correspondences. He then correlated the children's performance on all three tests.

His idea was that if there really are children who prefer to read by using a Phoenician strategy, then there should be a high correlation between performance on the regular words and the nonsense words: there should also be a lower correlation between the irregular words and the nonsense words. This is because nonsense words must be read phonologically and irregular words visually, and so if regular words are read on a phonological basis then the correlation between success in reading both regular and nonsense words should be high. This correlation should be higher than the one between nonsense words and irregular words, because the irregular words cannot be read phonologically and the nonsense words can only be read phonologically. Baron found that the first of these two correlations was indeed higher than the second, and subsequent work with his colleague Treiman has repeated this result several times (Baron, 1979, Treiman & Baron, 1981; Treiman, 1984).

Baron used exactly the same logic when looking for evidence for the Chinese (visual) strategy. There would have to be, he argued, a high correlation between performance in the regular and the irregular word list: the correlation between the irregular list and the nonsense words would have to be lower. His line of argument here is that irregular words can only be read visually and nonsense words only phonologically; therefore if children read words visually there should be a high correlation between their success on irregular and regular words because they can, in principle, read both kinds of word on a visual basis. However, the correlation between irregular words and nonsense words should be relatively low, because irregular words can be read on the basis of visual familiarity whereas nonsense words cannot. Baron also found that the first of these two correlations was indeed higher than the second, and this is a result that he and Treiman have also repeated in several studies. So they claim that they have evidence that children use both the Phoenician and the Chinese strategy.

However, their argument goes further than the claim that these two patterns simply establish the existence of both a Phoenician and a Chinese strategy. Baron and Treiman also claim that the pattern of correlations that they have discovered tells us a lot about differences between children. They argue (Baron & Treiman, 1980) that the very unevenness of the strength of the different correlations shows that there are considerable qualitative differences between children. If all the children used these two strategies to the same degree, they claim, then there would be no unevenness in the pattern of correlations, and the scores in all three lists would correlate with each other to the same extent. If there were no individual differences all children would rely on the same two strategies to the same degree, but the better children would use the two strategies more skilfully and so would do better on all three lists than the less successful children who would use the same strategies but less effectively. If this were the case then the correlation between performance on irregular words and on nonsense words would be quite high. But in fact Baron and Treiman have always shown it to be relatively low.

The argument is ingenious and persuasive. But it has its problems. Although the pattern of correlations allows Baron and Treiman to say that there must be Chinese and Phoenician readers, it does not provide us with a way of identifying which child is one kind of reader and which the other.

Treiman and Baron's use of nonsense words leads to another problem. It is true that the children had to use some form of a phonological code to read nonsense words, but which form? They may have read these words on a letter by letter basis, or they may have relied on sequences of letters which they connected to onsets and rimes. So there may have been Phoenicians among the children seen by Baron and Treiman, but we cannot say what kind of Phoenicians they were. Of course, at the time that the research was done, the influence of the two-route model was so strong that it was difficult to see that there might be more than one way to be a Phoenician. But it should be quite easy to incorporate the discovery that there are different kinds of phonological codes into a new study which takes advantage of Baron and Treiman's ingenious use of correlations.

Let us turn now to our main question about individual differences. Does the evidence for individual differences mean that a theory about the "normal" development of reading is unnecessary and inappropriate? There seem to us to be two options. One is that Baron and Treiman are wrong and that the differences that they have found simply reflect a developmental change. It may be the case that at the early stages of reading children read in a Chinese way and in later stages in a Phoenician way. In that case Baron and Treiman's results could simply have been due to some of their children being at the early stage and others at the later stage of reading.

On the other hand, Baron and Treiman's claim may be right. The children may all be at the same overall stage of reading, but some may read in one way and some in others. How does one decide between these two possibilities? We are afraid that there is nothing in Baron and Treiman's data that allows us to do so. They cannot dismiss the first possibility—that the differences are simply developmental ones, and the fact that they do not actually identify individual Chinese and Phoenician readers means that it is virtually impossible for them to do so. So for the moment we cannot accept, but nor can we disregard, these authors' interesting argument.

What is to be done? The only solution, it seems to us, is to find measures which will identify Chinese and Phoenician children and then apply these measures in a longitudinal study. If the developmental hypothesis is right all children will change, as they make more progress with reading, from one way of reading to the other—from Chinese to Phoenician or vice versa. If Baron and Treiman are right, some will adopt and stay with one form of reading, some with the other. Of course, such a study depends on our being able to find tests which will identify children who read visually, and children who read phonologically. But that should not be too difficult because many people have devised tests of this sort. Their aim, invariably, has been to look for differences among backward readers, but they could just as well be used with normal readers. Let us look at these tests and at the same time at the many claims for the existence of different types of backward reader.

DIFFERENCES AMONG POOR READERS

On the whole there has been surprisingly little work on differences among normal readers. A great deal more interest has been shown in differences in the ways in which individual backward readers read and spell. Here the argument takes a new turn. Invariably, the people who look for differences among backward readers end up making two quite separable claims. The first, and usually quite unexceptionable, claim is that some backward readers read and spell in one way, and some in quite another.

The second claim is much more controversial. It is that the different patterns of reading that one can detect in backward readers tell us a lot about the causes of their reading difficulties. Invariably it is assumed that the way that the backward reader sets about reading will tell us what is wrong with his reading. So, if some backward readers rely heavily on the phonological route, the reason for their reading difficulties is said to be an inability to take in visual cues. By the same token, if other backward readers depend on the visual route they must have been handicapped by not being able to take advantage of the phonological code.

One consequence of this second claim is that hypotheses about individual differences among backward readers are not at odds with the idea that there is only one normal course of development of reading. On the contrary, most people who write about different types of backwardness in reading emphatically agree with the idea of one normal path of development. They argue that the backward readers whom they study have fallen behind precisely because they have left this path, and they add the idea that some backward readers have diverged from the path in one direction, and some in another.

Group Studies

Our first example of a theory about individual differences is the well known account of them given by Eleanor Boder (1973). She claimed that some poor readers fall behind because of phonological difficulties, others because of visual difficulties, and still others because of a combination of these two kinds of problem. She called these three groups "dysphonetic readers", "dyseidetic readers", and "mixed readers". She based her claim for these three types of dyslexia on a study of the reading errors made by a group of 107 poor readers. The dysphonetic group made mainly phonetic errors ("rember" for "remember"), while the dyseidetic group made visual errors, such as being unable to recall the appearance of irregular words like "laugh". But these dyseidetic readers could analyse and read regular words on a letter-by-letter basis. The mixed group made both kinds of mistake.

Boder's study is well worth reading. It shows great clinical acumen, and the examples that she provided of children's reading and spelling mistakes are always interesting. She does not present statistics, but nonetheless her claim that these different subgroups exist has a definite ring of truth. We have only one worry about it. It concerns her assumption—one shared by many who followed the two-route model—that children can only read irregular words successfully if they read them as visual wholes. It takes very little reflection to see that this is not the only possibility. Let us take two very irregular words, "laugh" and "Gloucester". We cannot read either of them by applying grapheme-phoneme rules. Nor can we get very far with analogies, because there aren't any other words which contain the same spelling sequences and are pronounced in the same way. So we may indeed remember each of these two words by its visual appearance which in both cases is quite distinctive. But there is another possibility, which is that we remember the words as specific spelling sequences; that we learn that the letters l-a-u-g-h add up to "laugh". Boder does not consider this possibility (which, if it were true, would make her label "dyseidetic" quite inappropriate), and certainly does nothing to rule it out. We do not wish to dispute Boders' claim about finding different types of reading among children who have difficulty with reading, but we are not at all certain about her description of the dyseidetic group.

What about the second type of claim? Boder assumed that the differences that she found among children who were poor at reading provided the reason for their reading difficulties.

Boder did not report any research on normal children. She only studied differences among backward readers, and thus her claim that these differences tell us about the causes of their backwardness in reading is terribly suspect. Let us consider a ludicrous and entirely fictitious example to see why this is so. Suppose that someone studied the handwriting of a large group of children who were behind in spelling, and found that the slope of some of these children's writing was forward and of others backward. This person would be laughed out of court if he then argued that the basic problem behind the spelling difficulties of one group was that they wrote forward sloping words and of the other group that their words had a backward slope. People would see that this analysis is ridiculous because they know that children who have no spelling problems also often write either with a forward or with a backward slope.

In exactly the same way, we would have to abandon Boder's causal ideas if we found exactly the same patterns of reading among normal readers as she found in backward readers. The different patterns of reading could not be held to be a cause of reading difficulties if these same patterns are found in children who do not have these difficulties. So one has to make a comparison with normal readers, and Boder did not do that. That is why we cannot accept her causal claims. In fact we have already seen that Baron and Treiman have claimed that much the same subgroups exist among children who read normally for their age. If they are right, then Boder's second claim is quite unjustified. We need the equivalent data on normal children.

A few years later someone who was also interested in differences among backward readers ran a study which did involve a comparison with normal readers. But he chose the wrong normal readers. Mitterer (1982) gave a group of backward readers a series of tests which were meant to measure the children's dependence on phonological and visual codes. He claimed that some of the backward readers tended to read phonologically: they found it harder to read irregular words, which cannot be deciphered phonologically, than regular ones. Others seemed to him to be more dependent on visual cues: these children were badly thrown off course, for example, when they had to read words written in aLtErNaTiNg lower and upper case letters. mItTeReR, like Boder, made two claims. One is that there are differences among backward readers, and this seems indisputable to us. The other was that the reasons for children's difficulties can be traced back to the various patterns of reading that he had described. He based this second suggestion on a comparison with a group of normal readers. These were children of the same age as the backward readers and therefore well ahead of them in reading. Mitterer reported that he did not find the same pattern of differences in this second group, and therefore argued that the pattern that he had detected among the backward readers was confined to them and thus probably something to do with the reasons for their problems.

However, the fact that the reading level of the normal group was much higher than that of the backward readers makes this comparison meaningless. It is quite likely that patterns of individual differences take one form at one reading level and quite a different form at a higher level when children read different things and have had different experiences with reading. Mitterer should have made a reading level match when he chose his group of normal children.

Single Case Studies

The growing interest in differences among backward readers has led to a number of detailed "case studies" of individual dyslexic children. Most, although not all, of these have shown the influence of very similar studies of "acquired dyslexics"—adults who were able to read quite normally until they suffered some form of brain damage. The connection between research on acquired dyslexia and case studies of developmental dyslexia—of children who have had difficulties with reading ever since they began to be taught to read—involves more than just a common method. The people who have done these studies usually believe that the difficulties suffered by acquired dyslexics and by developmental dyslexics are much the same.

It is quite clear that there are different forms of acquired dyslexia. In fact, the differences among these adult patients provided the best evidence that could be found for the two-route model. One type of acquired dyslexia is called phonological dyslexia. It refers to people who apparently have great difficulty with the phonological code. They can hardly read nonsense words. They do not on the whole find regular words any easier to read than irregular ones, and the reason often given for this is that they read regular and irregular words visually, and so whether the relationship between letters and sounds in any word is regular or not makes no difference to them. They have great difficulty with long and unfamiliar regular words, like "herpetology". All in all these people are very like the children Boder described as "dysphonetic" (Fig. 8.1).

Another form of acquired dyslexia is called surface dyslexia. These are people who read in a very different way. They apparently have little difficulty with the phonological code, but do not seem to be able to use "the visual route". They find regular words (short or long) quite easy and irregular ones extremely difficult. Once again Boder's model comes to mind, for these people fit her "dyseidetic" category well.

The claim has now been made that there are also "phonological" and "surface" *developmental* dyslexics. This need not surprise us, because Boder had already made

	Phonological dyslexic (Reads visually)	Surface dyslexic (Reads phonologically)
Regular words	Reads if short Stumbles if long	Reads easily
Irregular words	Reads as well as regular words	Rarely reads
Nonsense words	Unable to read	Reads easily
Errors	Visual: "camp" for "cape" "weight" for "weigh"	Regularisations: "steek" for "steak

FIG. 8.1.   The contrasting patterns of impairment in phonological and surface dyslexia.

the same claim, although with different words, when she distinguished "dysphonetic" from "dyseidetic" dyslexic children. But the case studies which led to the claim about phonological and surface developmental dyslexics deserve attention, because they produced some genuinely new observations.

Temple and Marshall (1983) described a 17 year old girl (HM) with a reading level of 10 years, who seemed to them to read in much the same way as a typical adult "phonological dyslexic". The girl found it almost impossible to read nonsense words, and also long regular words like "herpetology". She made "visual paralexic" errors (e.g. reading "camp" for "cape") and derivational errors ("weight" for "weigh") which seemed to show that she depended heavily on recognising the appearance of a word in order to be able to read it, and the notion that she was relying on a visual strategy to read was further supported by the finding that she read irregular words as easily as regular ones. Temple and Marshall concluded that the girl's main problem was a phonological one. They then argued that this phonological weakness was the cause of her reading problems. This same causal claim was made again by Marshall (1984).

The second study was also based on a 17 year old girl (CD) with a reading level of 10 years, and was reported by M. Coltheart, Masterson, Byng, Prior and Riddoch, (1983). The symptoms shown by this girl were almost a mirror image of those shown by Temple and Marshall's dyslexic. She could read regular words much more easily than irregular ones, and made regularisation errors, which result from over-applying phonological rules so that irregular words are pronounced as though they are regular (e.g. "steek" for "steak"). She also made stress errors, which involve reading the word with the correct pronunciation, but with the stress on the wrong syllable and while reading, she produced some entirely new words ("neologisms"). M. Coltheart et al. pointed out that these are exactly the symptoms that are found in adult "surface dyslexics". The authors argued that the girl's problem lay in recognising familiar words.

She had difficulty, they argued, in using either a visual or an orthographic strategy. Instead, like surface dyslexics, she had to rely on letter-sound correspondences to read every word which she encountered.

We have mentioned the similarity between the ideas of Eleanor Boder on the one hand and the link which Temple and Marshall and M. Coltheart make with acquired dyslexia on the other. There is a common empirical weakness too, because these two case studies, interesting and ingenious though they are, contained no comparisons with normal children. Therefore the assumption which pervades both studies—that the authors are describing some unusual pattern of reading which provides the reason for these particular children's reading difficulties—is quite unjustified. The authors should have checked that these same patterns of reading are not to be found among normal readers at the same level of reading.

It has been shown since (Bryant & Impey, 1986) that all but one of the "symptoms" demonstrated in these two girls are found to an equal extent in some normal children who read quite normally. These authors worked with a group of children with a mean reading age of 10 years 1 month, and gave them most of the tests used by Temple and Marshall and by M. Coltheart et al. The tasks included reading regular and irregular words, reading long regular words, and a number of nonsense word reading tasks of the kind used in both previous studies.

It turned out that most of the mistakes made by Temple and Marshall's phonological dyslexic and by M. Coltheart et al.'s surface dyslexic were made by these normal readers as well. Let us look at the "phonological" symptoms first. Bryant and Impey found that their normal readers were better at reading nonsense words than HM, the dyslexic girl studied by Temple and Marshall. However, the normal readers behaved in much the same way as did HM when it came to visual paralexias and derivational errors. Some of the normal children actually made more of these errors than HM had.

Surface dyslexic symptoms also abounded. The normal readers found regular words harder to read than irregular ones, as CD, the surface dyslexic studied by M. Coltheart et al. had done, and three children actually showed a greater discrepancy between regular and irregular words than CD did. Six children made more regularisation errors than CD, and the mean percentage of neologisms made by the group was almost identical to the number of CD's neologisms.

It looks as though the pattern of mistakes which were found in the two detailed case studies are not at all unusual. They seem to be characteristic of children of that reading level. That means, of course, that these patterns cannot be used as a basis for a theory about the causes of the backward readers' difficulties.

Bryant and Impey (1986) also found differences among the normal readers. Some were more like HM, others more like CD. A factor analysis showed that one common factor accounted for 67.9% of the variance in reading, and that the phonological symptoms were strongly negatively loaded on this factor, while the surface symptoms were strongly positively loaded. This suggests striking qualitative differences between normal readers, and underlines the point that these differences cannot be used to explain the difficulties of the dyslexic children. The analysis agrees well with Baron and Treiman's Phoenician/Chinese distinction.

Bryant and Impey's study involved only normal readers. Another study by Baddeley, Logie and Ellis (1988) also dealt with the possibility of a connection between acquired and surface dyslexia, but this included a direct comparison between a group of developmental dyslexics and two control groups of normal readers, one with the same reading age and the other with the same chronological age as the dyslexic group. The children had to read lists of regular and irregular words and also of nonsense words. Once again, normal as well as dyslexic children made more mistakes when they read nonsense words than real words, and regular words than irregular ones. These two effects were no stronger in the dyslexic group than in the reading age-matched control group. The authors concluded, as Bryant and Impey had done, that the symptoms characteristic of various kinds of acquired dyslexia do not provide an explanation for developmental dyslexia.

Another study of individual differences in backward readers was published at about the same time by Seymour (1986). His approach also was heavily influenced by previous work on acquired dyslexia, but his methods were quite different from those of Temple and Marshall and of M. Coltheart et al. He used techniques drawn from cognitive psychology, such as reaction time measures, and he also had a normal control group. Seymour's idea was to test a model about three "routes" to reading. One was the "grapheme-phoneme" route, another was a route from morphemes to whole words, and the third from morphemes to sounds. The first involves reading on the basis of letter-sound correspondences, the second the recognition of words as visual wholes, and the third the recognition of morphemes which represent sounds (such as "jump" in "jumped" and "jumping").

Seymour's idea was that impairment in any one of these three routes could lead to dyslexia, and that different children might have different problems with different routes. So a child whose grapheme-phoneme route was impaired would have particular difficulty reading nonsense words. Similarly, a child whose morphemic-semantic route was impaired would have difficulty with lexical decision tasks (deciding whether a string of letters is a word or not) involving time constraints.

Seymour gave 21 dyslexic children and 13 control children a large battery of tests in order to pick up difficulties in either of the three routes. The dyslexic children were older than the normal children, but there was a discrepancy too in reading age: the mean reading age of the normal children was 12 years 4 months, while that of the backward children was 10 years 4 months. All but one of the normal children had a reading age higher than 12 years, while only eight of the 21 backward readers were at this level.

Seymour claims to have found evidence for specific impairments through the entire range in his group. However, the fact that 13 of the backward group had much lower reading levels than that of the normal readers means that we cannot be sure that their performance really indicated any impairment. We have to concentrate on the remaining eight backward readers, but two of them showed only very mild impairments, and did not appear to be different in any way from the normal children. That left six backward readers. One of them was worse on every kind of test, visual and phonological, than the normal control group, and so did not show any specific deficit. Of the remaining five, three appeared to have difficulty with the tests of grapheme-phoneme skills. As the main measure here was of reading nonsense words, this result is consistent with previous work which shows that many poor readers have difficulties with this kind of test. That leaves two backward readers, and Seymour claimed that both of them suffered from a visual impairment. His main evidence for this was that their speed in matching words visually was very slow. This claim to have discovered two visual dyslexics is a striking one. It is, as far as we know, the first time that a reading age match has produced evidence of a visual impairment among some dyslexic children. However, the claim must be treated with great caution, because we cannot be certain that the difficulty is specifically visual. After all, the tests involved written words, and the backward readers' difficulty could be the result of a problem with words rather than with visual material *per se*. If this were a genuine visual deficit, then these two children should have had difficulty matching other visual material, such as different shapes and patterns, as well as written words. Surely these two children and any others like them should be given this crucial test as well.

SPELLING DIFFICULTIES AND INDIVIDUAL DIFFERENCES

If children read in different ways, do they spell differently from each other too? Treiman (1984) has claimed that there are also differences in the way that children spell words. Again, most of the relevant research is about children with reading and spelling difficulties. However, Treiman has claimed that normal children can be classified as Phoenician and Chinese spellers. Her evidence comes from a study of some 9 and 10 year old children which took much the same form as her and Baron's previous work on differences in children's reading.

She gave these children three sets of words to read, and another three sets to spell. The three spelling lists involved words that were regular ("gum"), exception ("some") or nonsense ("fum"), from the point of view of the way in which the sound of the word was spelled. The children also had to read regular "dome", exception ("come") and nonsense ("gome") words.

Treiman found the same pattern of correlations with the different spelling lists as she and Baron had previously found with reading (and she also found that same pattern of reading correlations as before). So she concluded that there are Phoenician and Chinese spellers as well as readers. We react to this conclusion in the same way that we did to the earlier conclusion about reading. We need further longitudinal work to be sure that Treiman was not simply picking up a developmental difference.

There has also been some research on individual differences in the spelling patterns of children who are backward in reading and in spelling. Most of this has taken the form of detailed case studies. An example is a report by Temple (1986) of two children with severe reading and spelling problems. One of the advantages of this study is that Temple did compare these two children to others who had no problems with reading and spelling. Both children were 10 years old, but had a spelling age of around 7 years. One was a girl who could read regular words and nonsense words quite well, but made many mistakes when she tried to read irregular words (M. Coltheart et al.'s "surface pattern"). The other was a boy who could read irregular words as well as regular ones, but had great difficulty with nonsense words (Temple and Marshall's "phonological" pattern). Temple asked them to spell a list of 160 words, and she also asked a group of 7 year old children to do the same. Thus she, quite rightly, made a spelling level match.

Her main interest was in the phonological "plausibility" of the children's mistakes. We have seen how even very young children can produce a completely incorrect spelling which nevertheless sounds right ("noys", "kwyit"). Temple judged a mistake as a plausible spelling if, when "the errors were read aloud, they would be homophonic with the target"(p. 84).

She found a considerable difference between the two cases. Most of the girl's mistakes were plausible ones ("fier", "agektif", "orkestrer", "cemist"); the boy, in striking contrast, made very few mistakes of this sort. At times, Temple's judgements about the plausibility seem quite tough to us. For example, she does not allow "throt" as a plausible spelling for the word "throat"; yet the boy was probably thinking of the sound of the letter name for "o"—as normal five year old children often do (see Chapter 3)—in which case this would have been a decent phonological representation of the sound of the word. However, the difference between the two children was so large that we are convinced by Temple's argument that the boy did not apply a phonological code to spelling or did not apply it nearly so much as the other child did. She also reported that the girl's spelling was in line with the normal children's, but that the boy's was not. He made far fewer plausible spelling mistakes than did any of the 10 normal readers and spellers with whom he was compared.

Temple's conclusion is convincing. It does seem that the boy who made so few plausible mistakes spelled in a way that was qualitatively different from other children who were at the same spelling level, and different too from at least one other backward speller. This particular boy also seemed to be insensitive to rhyme. He could not produce rhymes at all well and he made many mistakes when he was asked to recognise rhyme. Temple argued that this was further evidence that the boy was insensitive to phonological segments, but we think that this particular observation raises another question. Was this boy generally insensitive phonologically or was his main difficulty with rhyme and consequently with onset and rime?

There is another interesting report of a similar case of a child of eight years with a spelling age of six years. Snowling, Stackhouse and Rack (1986) found that this child had difficulties with "input phonology": he found it difficult to judge whether two words that he heard spoken, one after the other, were the same or not. His judgements about rhyme were also often wrong. The spelling mistakes made by this child were often as implausible as those made by the boy in Temple's study who also produced implausible spellings. He wrote "mupter" for "trap" and "aurbrella" for "umbrella". If there is a normal path of development of spelling, there seems no reason to doubt that these two children who produced such idiosyncratic spellings departed from it at an early stage.

CONCLUSIONS

There are two reasons why we need to know if there are individual differences in the way that children read. One is that we cannot assess the importance of differences among backward readers unless we know whether these patterns also exist among normal readers. The other concerns theories about reading. Should we stick to the idea of one pathway, or not?

So far the question of individual differences among normal children is an open one. Baron and Treiman certainly did demonstrate qualitative differences among children of the same age, but these might have been developmental differences nonetheless.

However, we certainly cannot dismiss Baron and Treiman's idea, and if it is right many of the claims that have been made about individual differences among backward readers are misguided. Differences in patterns of reading among these children will only tell us about the reasons for reading difficulties if the same patterns do not exist in normal children. Several authors did not take the precaution of checking whether the patterns that they were describing were unusual (i.e. not to be found in normal children), and subsequent work has shown that these patterns do occur in normal children too.

On the other hand, there is some evidence of highly unusual types of spelling in some children with spelling problems. Some of these children spell in a way that has not been seen in normal children.

In the next chapter we shall deal with theories about "normal" development in reading. It seems to us that there are enough data to show that any satisfactory theory must cope with the possibility of children learning to read and to spell in different ways.

CHAPTER 9

Theories about Learning
to Read

TWO REQUIREMENTS FOR A
DEVELOPMENTAL THEORY

We have been discussing the changes that take place in young children's phonological skills and in their understanding of written language. We have already made several claims about these developmental changes and we think that these claims add up to a theory—to a developmental theory. It is time now to pull the various strands of our argument together and to say what this theory is.

Any theory about developmental changes has two jobs to do. One is to say exactly what form the developmental changes take. What new skills has the child acquired? What can he or she understand now that eluded him or her completely two months ago? These are the *first* questions that the theorist must answer, and they are not as simple as they seem at first. It is not just a matter, for example, of saying that children of seven can now read a lot of words which were too difficult for them a year ago. We need to know if the seven year old has acquired some underlying skill which makes it possible for him or her to read the new words. "Underlying" is the important word here. Theories about developmental changes have to explain the underlying nature of these changes. If we remark that children get much better at reading unfamiliar regular words between the ages of seven and eight years, we are not making a theoretical statement: we are simply describing a developmental change. Our account becomes a theoretical one if we argue that at seven years children acquire some new skill (such as being able to break words up into phonemes) which allows them to read more regular words.

But we also have to ask what causes children to acquire new, underlying skills. This is the *second* requirement for any theory about development: the theory must provide an answer to causal questions. You cannot understand a system that is constantly changing unless you know something about the reasons for these changes. There are pressing practical reasons too for finding out about the factors that lead to changes in children's reading and spelling. We cannot give any coherent advice about how to teach children to read unless we know what prompts the changes: nor can we be much help to children who are finding it hard to learn to read.

We mention these two requirements because, on the whole, theories about the development of reading have coped a great deal better with the first of them than with the second. Causal questions are always the hardest to answer, and so far theoretical accounts of children's reading have not made much progress with them. One of the main aims of this chapter will be to make a start at giving an account of the causal factors that affect children's reading. But we shall begin by discussing some other people's theories before we set out our own ideas about the development of reading and its causes.

MARSH'S FOUR STAGES

We dealt with some of George Marsh's research on children's attempts to read and spell words that are entirely new to them (Chapter 4). In his theoretical account of this research Marsh argued, quite rightly in our view, that one should not look just at children's reading. Children who are learning to read have certain intellectual skills and these too are changing as they grow up. Marsh thought that the form of children's reading must be heavily influenced by the stage of intellectual development that they happen to be at. So he turned to Piaget's well-known theory of intellectual development and suggested that there are distinct stages in children's reading, just as there are distinct stages of intellectual development according to Piaget. Marsh also claimed that the stage that any child had reached in reading was determined by the stage of intellectual development that he or she happened to be at.

There are, Marsh suggested, four main stages in the development of reading (see Fig. 9.1).

Stage 1.   When children begin to read, they learn "rote associations" between "an unsynthesised visual stimulus and an unanalyzed oral response" (Marsh, Friedman, Desberg & Saterdahl, 1981, p.201). They read words as logograms, and this of course has the disadvantage that they have no rational way of working out what an unfamiliar written word means. As for the use of a phonological code, that is out of the question. "Children in the first stage find it very difficult to decenter from the unanalyzed oral response to perform such tasks as phonemic segmentation" (Marsh et al., 1981, p.201).

The phrase "difficult to decenter" is an important one, for that is Marsh's link with Piaget's theory. Piaget argued that one of the main intellectual difficulties of children of this age was that they tend to focus their attention on prominent details and cannot analyse patterns into separate parts.

Stage 2.   Two major changes happen here. The child begins to use context in combination with linguistic cues to help him or her to read, and he or she also begins

Stage	Strategy	Responses
1. Linguistic substitution	Rote learning	See "boy", read "boy"
	Linguistic guessing	See "The cime went to..." Read "The boy went to..."
2. Discrimination Net substitution	Rote learning	See "boy", read "boy"
	Visually similar guessing	See "cime", read "cats"
	Linguistic and visual guessing	See "The cime went to..." Read "The child went to..."
3. Sequential decoding	Rote learning	See "boy", read "boy"
	Decoded letter-by-letter	See "cime", read "kime"
4. Hierarchical decoding	Higher order rules	See "cime", read "sim"
	Analogies	See "faugh", read "faff"

FIG. 9.1.   Marsh's (1980) four-stage theory of reading development.

to make rudimentary analogies by spotting similarites between new words and familiar ones. So shown the word "cime" in isolation children say "cats", but shown it in context preceded by "the", they will say "the child".

Stage 3.   By this time (at the age of about eight years) children are well into what Piaget called the concrete operations period. This means, according to Piaget, that they are beginning to be able to master quite complex rules. Marsh claims that as a result children are now able to use "combinatorial rules" (another Piagetian phrase) in order to analyse words into phonemes, and to use grapheme-phoneme correspondences to "decode" new words. In this stage children "can decode new words if they are regular" (Marsh et al., 1981, p.205).

Stage 4.   At this final stage children begin to be able to use "higher order" rules, such as "the letter 'c' is pronounced /s/ when followed by i, e, and y". This rule is said to be a higher order one because it is a conditional rule: the pronunciation of the letter "c" is conditional on the following vowel. This is the stage when children begin to make proper analogies when they read. "Although the strategy may be available early in the stage of concrete operations, it is not used spontaneously to any great extent until much later in development" (Marsh & Desberg, 1983, p. 152). Again we have to turn to Piaget for a reason why analogies come so late. Piaget argued that analogies involve a kind of reasoning which children cannot master until after the age of 10 years (Piaget & Inhelder, 1958).

How does Marsh's scheme stand up to the data (much of which was gathered after Marsh originally produced his theory) that we have reviewed in this book? It seems to us that the evidence agrees with the theory on some points but not on others. His suggestion that children originally treat written words as logograms fits well with the facts. His claim that it is some time before children rely on grapheme-phoneme rules has also received a lot of support from subsequent research. The importance which Marsh attributed to analogies in reading seems, from the data that we reviewed in Chapter 4, to be entirely justified. In all these ways the theory has proved to be a remarkably successful one.

However, the theory has the weakness (shared by most accounts of children's reading) that it confines itself to phonemes when it deals with phonological awareness, and to grapheme-phoneme correspondences when it deals with phonological codes in reading. This has two consequences. One is that the children's early phonological skills, such as their awareness of rhyme, are ignored in Marsh's scheme. The second and related problem is that children's associations between speech units like rimes and sequences of letters form no part of the theory. In Chapter 4 we showed that these associations are also important in young children's reading, and make it possible for them to read many new words by analogy.

Marsh's theory deals with reading. It would not provide a good account of children's spelling since there is no evidence for an early logographic stage in spelling. In fact, the data on early spelling and particularly on invented spelling are actually evidence against Marsh's theory because they show that children can use "combinatorial rules" about letter-sound relationships at a very early stage.

The upshot is that Marsh's theory is a good start but is not viable in its present form, because it does not deal with children's sensitivity to onset and rime or with their reliance on a phonological code in spelling. Marsh's use of Piaget's theory as a source of ideas about the causes of reading development is interesting, but the causal links are vague particularly when the theory deals with letter-sound associations. "We know little about the exact factors in instruction which produce a shift from Stage 2 to Stage 3. The term "phonics" covers a multitude of techniques" (Marsh et al., 1981, p. 205). Piaget had nothing directly to say about phonological awareness, and Marsh's theory seems itself to be too vague on that particular subject.

FRITH'S THREE PHASES AND SIX STEPS

Uta Frith (1985), whose work on reading and spelling we have mentioned in several parts of this book, devised a three-stage theory of reading. She used Marsh's account but revised it in several ways.

Her three stages were: (1) logographic; (2) alphabetic; and (3) orthographic. In the first stage children read words as logograms, in the second they also apply grapheme-phoneme rules, and in the third they begin as well to analyse words "into orthographic units without phonological conversion". Development here involves adding strategies. One strategy does not supplant another. Children who have reached the end of this developmental sequence have at their disposal all the strategies associated with each of the stages and they use all of them.

The first two stages of the sequence are clear. The last needs more attention. Frith's claim about the orthographic stage is that children begin to recognise "strings" of letters which "can be used to create by recombination an almost unlimited number of words" (1985, p. 308). So Frith's idea is that children move from analysing words letter by letter to recognising and using sequences of letters. Her claim that this happens without "phonological conversion" puzzles us. Letter sequences like -"ight" must be part of Frith's scheme, and they represent sounds.

We have another point to make about this last stage. Marsh and Frith talk about orthographic strategies in different ways. Marsh concentrates on quite sophisticated conditional rules, and Frith on memory for spelling sequences. This difference should be recognised. It is certainly important as far as our own ideas are concerned. We accept Marsh's view that children take some time to learn conditional orthographic rules, but we do not agree with Frith's ideas about spelling sequences, because some of the evidence that we discussed in Chapter 4 suggests that children recognise and use these sequences at a very early stage in reading.

On the whole Frith's scheme seems an economical account of the facts. However, it provides no answers to any causal questions and, as Frith pointed out, it does not explain the differences that we have noted (Chapter 3) between reading and spelling. As Frith has done more than anyone to draw our attention to the differences between reading and spelling, it was natural that she should adapt her theory to deal with these differences. This led to a new "six-step" model (Fig.9.2).

In this model the logographic stage again precedes the alphabetic stage both in reading and in spelling. But children take to the logographic code more quickly when they read than when they write words, and the child's experience of reading words as

Step	Reading	Writing
1a	Logographic 1	(Symbolic)
1b	Logographic 2	Logographic 2
2a	Logographic 2	Alphabetic 1
2b	Alphabetic 2	Alphabetic 2
3a	Orthographic 1	Alphabetic 3
3b	Orthographic 2	Orthographic 2

Note. "1" signifies a very basic level of the skill, "2" a more advanced level, and so on.

FIG. 9.2.   Frith's (1985) six-step theory.

logograms eventually helps him or her to use the same code more effectively when he or she spells. The causal links go the other way round with the alphabetic code. Children use it first when they spell, and their experiences of spelling words alphabetically eventually have the effect of showing them how to read alphabetically as well. The direction of cause and effect is reversed again when we come to the orthographic code. Children use the code first when they read and later, as a result, when they spell.

So Frith's model provides an account of the differences between reading and spelling and it also suggests some causal links. But cause and effect are confined to factors "within" the model. Experiences with reading affect the way children spell, and experiences with spelling influence their reading. Frith does not share Marsh's concern with children's experiences and skills outside the world of reading.

So the causal side of both theories seems incomplete to us. Marsh's link with Piagetian intellectual stages is unsatisfactory because it is vague about phonology and it cannot cope with differences between reading and spelling. Frith's model tells us little about the effects of skills, particularly phonological skills, which children acquire before they learn to read.

We have one other concern about Frith's model—a worry that we have already expressed about Marsh's. It is about her suggestion that children spell logographically before they spell alphabetically. We know of no evidence for this claim, and much of the data that we reviewed in Chapter 3 seems to be good evidence against it.

We can summarise our conclusions about Marsh's and Frith's theories quite briefly. The claim made by both of them that children read logographically first and alphabetically later seems to us to have been entirely justified by later research. So has Marsh's idea that children learn complex, conditional rules about orthography at an even later stage. But the claim that children spell logographically before they spell alphabetically—again made by Marsh and by Frith—does not seem to fit any of the facts. Both theories too seem to us to be too narrow in their discussion about phonological awareness, as they mention only phoneme awareness and grapheme -phoneme correspondence. The fact that Marsh and Frith ignore rhyme and the awareness of onset and rime probably also accounts for the apparent reluctance of both of them to suggest that children recognise sequences of letters and relate them to sounds at a relatively early stage in reading.

A THEORY ABOUT CAUSES

In this book we have been constructing a different kind of theory. It is not a theory about stages, for we do not think that children take a series of discrete and identifiable steps when they learn to read and to spell. Our theory concentrates on causal connections: only these, we think, can explain the course of reading and spelling, and why some children make quicker progress than others, and why there might be qualitative differences in the way that children read. Let us then start with the causal factors. We think that there are three main causal factors to consider.

1. Pre-school Phonological Skills—Rhyme and Alliteration

Children are sensitive to the sounds in words long before they learn to read, and they also categorise words by their sounds. But these sounds are not phonemes, or at any rate not always phonemes. The important phonological units for young children are onset and rime. The phonological skill that they bring to reading and writing is the ability to divide a word into its onset and its rime, and also to categorise words which have the same onset or the same rime.

The effect of this skill on their progress in reading is considerable both in a quantitative and in a qualitative sense. Children who are sensitive to rhyme eventually do much better at reading (although not at mathematics), and children who are taught about rhyme are more successful at reading than those who are not given this training. This shows that there is a link between children's awareness of rhyme and alliteration and their progress in reading. But the link itself explains quite a lot about the way that young children read.

There is precious little evidence that young children use grapheme-phoneme relations when they read words. But it is another matter when we come to onsets and rimes. These are represented in fairly consistent ways in writing. In fact, the representation of rimes by sequences of letters is certainly a great deal more reliable than the representation of phonemes by single letters. Our evidence suggests that right from the start, and perhaps with very little explicit instruction to do so, children learn to associate onsets and rimes with strings of letters.

One of the most interesting results of this early sensitivity to onsets and rimes is that children make inferences or analogies about new words on the basis of spelling patterns in words that they already know, and that they do this as soon as they begin to read. These inferences are the main phonological activity that we have been able to discern in the early stages of reading. Children also make them when they spell.

So our first causal link begins with events that take place some time before children begin to learn to read. They hear, and produce, rhyme. They become adept at recognising when words have common rimes or common onsets. So they form categories of words and when they begin to read they soon recognise that words in the same categories often have spelling patterns in common and that this spelling sequence represents the common sound. As soon as they realise this, they can make inferences about new words, and they do.

Our belief that the children are sophisticated enough to form spelling categories and to make inferences about spelling sequences as soon as they begin to read, is one of the reasons why we do not wish to suggest a series of discrete stages in the development of reading. We think that a great deal of the development takes the form of children just getting gradually better at strategies which they use right from the start. Our data suggest that they make inferences at the beginning but not often and not all that successfully. As they become more experienced they become much better at getting these inferences right.

2. Instruction and Phonemes

The experience of coming to grips with an alphabetic script—our second causal factor—has an enormous effect on children's awareness of sounds. Children begin to detect and recognise phonemes as a direct result of being taught to read and write such a script.

There are, it is true, other ways of becoming aware of phonemes than by learning about an alphabet, as Mann's work shows. But there is no doubt that for children of five and six years of age the experience of being taught to read and spell is an extremely effective way to learn about phonemes. Moreover, the effects are rather rapid. Our own longitudinal work showed that, very soon after beginning to read, children become able to break up rimes into phonemes. But they do not apply their new-found awareness to reading. Here is a great irony: the experience of being taught to read introduces children to phonemes, and yet their new knowledge of phonemes seems at first to play little part in their reading.

But this new knowledge does have an immediate effect. Children use it when they spell. They adopt a "phonemic" code as soon as they begin to write words. Onset and rime also play a part in children's early spelling, as we have seen, but these units rub shoulders with their smaller brethren, phonemes.

So at first there is a discrepancy and a separation between children's reading and spelling. It is still not clear why children are so willing to break up words into phonemes when they write, and yet are so reluctant to think in terms of phonemes when they read. But there can be little doubt that at first children's reading and spelling are different and separate. The most dramatic demonstration of this separation is the fact that young children often cannot read some words which they know how to spell and also fail to spell some words which they can read.

3. Spelling and Reading

The third causal link in our theory was originally suggested by Uta Frith. It is the link between children's reading and their spelling. Here, cause and effect travel in both directions. We suggest that the experiences which children have while reading influence the way that they spell, and that their knowledge of spelling affects their reading.

This third claim is the nearest that we get to a stage theory, for here we are suggesting a qualitative change. Qualitative changes played no part in our ideas about the importance of children's awareness of onset and rime, and the effects of instruction on the detection of phonemes. There, we dealt with influences which are in play as soon as children begin to read and spell. As time goes by children get better at linking spelling sequences with onsets and rimes and at manipulating phonemes, but these are quantitative changes in our view. On the other hand, we find definite signs of a qualitative shift when we look at the relations between reading and spelling.

Our point about the shift is simple. At first when children begin to read and to spell words they make hardly any connection between these two activities. They carry them out in rather different ways, and they often seem unable to use their knowledge about reading to help them spell a word, or their knowledge about a word's spelling to help them to read it. Later on, after roughly two years' experience of learning to read, they begin to connect reading and spelling. One consequence of their making this connection is that they no longer specialise. They no longer confine global strategies to reading, and they are readier than before to use their awareness of sounds when they read as well as when they spell words. Thus, at around this time there are qualitative changes in the ways that they read and spell.

We have to admit that this idea is still speculative. There is still a lot of work to be done on the relationship between reading and spelling, and in particular we need to know more about the initial separation between the two activities. Why does it happen in the first place? Does it help children make sense of reading and spelling? We do not know, but longitudinal work and studies of the effect of different kinds of teaching could provide the answer.

LATER DEVELOPMENTS

We think that Marsh's claim, that children do not learn complex, conditional orthographic rules till quite late on, is plausible. There is very little evidence on this kind of learning (Guthrie & Seifert, 1977). We do know that the development of phonological awareness continues during this stage as well. Some of the more difficult phonological tasks, such as Bruce's phoneme deletion task, continue to cause children difficulties up to the age of around nine and ten years. However, we know little about the connection between this kind of development and the way that children learn the conditional orthographic rules that play such an important part in the final stage of Marsh's theory.

Marsh turned to children's cognitive development when he looked for the major influence on children's ability to understand and use these rules. Another possibility is that children's phonological skills also play a part. After all, these are rules about the relationship between sounds and alphabetic letters, and so the phonological connection might be important here as well.

There is a way in which children's phonological skills could lead them to an understanding of these rules. If categories play the early and important part that we think that they do in children's reading, it is quite likely that children in the end will form higher order categories—categories of categories—as well. For example, when they are thoroughly familiar with "-ite" words and "-ile" words and "-ise" words, they may then put these three categories together into a super-category of "-i*e" words, all of which have the same long vowel sound. They may also form an "-a*e" category which tells them the same kind of thing about the long "a" sound. Finally, they could construct an even more abstract category of "-VCe" words—words that end in a "vowel-consonant-final 'e'" sequence. This category tells them in effect that the final "e" lengthens the preceding vowel. So the formation of categories which is such an important part of the early stages of reading could also lay the basis for the acquisition of more complex and abstract orthographic rules which takes place several years after children begin to learn to read.

We think that this is an exciting idea, and a good example of the power of phonological theories about children's reading. We hope that we have convinced you that theories about children's phonological skills and their reading have produced many good ideas, and also that they have been responsible for some of the most interesting and ingenious experimental research that has ever been done with children.

References

Alegria, J., Pignot, E. & Morais, J. (1982). Phonetic analysis of speech and memory codes in beginning readers. *Memory and Cognition, 10,* 451–556.

Backman, J., Bruck, M., Hebert, M. & Seidenberg, M.S. (1984). Acquisition and use of spelling-sound information in reading. *Journal of Experimental Child Psychology, 38,* 114–133.

Baddeley, A.D., Logie, R.H. & Ellis, N.C. (1988). Characteristics of developmental dyslexia. *Cognition, 29,* 197–228.

Baddeley, A.D., Ellis N.C., Miles T.R. & Lewis V.J. (1982). Developmental and acquired dyslexia: a comparison. *Cognition, 11,* 185–199.

Baron, J. (1977). Mechanisms for pronouncing printed words: use and acquisition. In D. LaBerge and S.J. Samuels (Eds), *Basic processes in reading: perception and comprehension* (pp. 175–216). Hillsdale, N.J.: Lawrence Erlbaum Associates Inc.

Baron, J. (1979). Orthographic and word specific mechanisms in children's reading of words. *Child Development, 50,* 60–72.

Baron, J. & Treiman, R. (1980). Some problems in the study of differences in cognitive processes. *Memory and Cognition, 8,* 313–321.

Barron, R. (1980). Visual and phonological strategies in reading and spelling. In U. Frith (Ed.), *Cognitive processes in spelling* (pp. 195–213). London: Academic Press.

Barron, R. (1986). Word recognition in early reading: A review of the direct and indirect access hypotheses. *Cognition, 24,* 93–119.

Barron, R. & Baron, J. (1977). How children get meaning from printed words. *Child Development, 48,* 587–594.

Beech, J.R. & Harding, L.M. (1984). Phonemic processing and the poor reader from the developmental point of view. *Reading Research Quarterly, 19,* 357–366.

Bertelson, P., Morais, J., Alegria J. & Content A. (1985). Phonetic analysis capacity and learning to read. *Nature*, *313*, 73–74.

Berthoud-Papandropoulou, I. (1978). An experimental study of children's ideas about language. In A. Sinclair, R.J. Jarvella and W.J.M. Levelt (Eds), *The child's conception of language* (pp. 55–64). Berlin: Springer.

Besner, D. (1987). Phonology, lexical access in reading, & articulatory suppression: a critical review. *Quarterly Journal of Experimental Psychology*, *39A*, 467–578.

Bisanz, G.L., Das, J.P. & Mancini, G. (1984). Children's memory for phonemically confusable and nonconfusable letters: Changes with age and reading ability. *Child Development*, *55*, 1845–1854.

Boder, E. (1973). Developmental dyslexia: a diagnostic approach based on three atypical reading-spelling patterns. *Developmental Medicine and Child Neurology*, *15*, 663–687.

Bowey, J.A. & Patel, R.K. (1988). Metalinguistic ability and early reading achievement. *Applied Psycholinguistics*, *9*, 367–383.

Bradley, L. & Bryant, P.E. (1978). Difficulties in auditory organisation as a possible cause of reading backwardness. *Nature*, *271*, 746–747.

Bradley, L. & Bryant, P.E. (1979). The independence of reading and spelling in backward and normal readers. *Developmental Medicine and Child Neurology*, *21*, 504–514.

Bradley, L. & Bryant, P.E. (1983). Categorising sounds and learning to read—a causal connection. *Nature*, *301*, 419–521.

Bradley L. & Bryant P.E. (1985). *Rhyme and Reason in Reading and Spelling*. I.A.R.L.D. Monographs No. 1. Ann Arbor: University of Michigan Press.

Bruce, D.J. (1964). The analysis of word sounds. *British Journal of Educational Psychology*, *34*, 158–170.

Bruck, M. (1988). The word recognition and spelling of dyslexic children. *Reading Research Quarterly*, *23*, 51–69.

Bruck, M. & Treiman, R. (1989). *Phonological awareness and spelling in normal children and dyslexics: The case of initial consonant clusters*. Unpublished manuscript.

Bruck, M. & Waters, G. (1988). An analysis of the spelling errors of children who differ in their reading and spelling skills. *Applied Psycholinguistics*, *9*, 77–92.

Bryant, P.E. & Bradley, L. (1980). Why children sometimes write words which they cannot read. In U. Frith (Ed.) *Cognitive processes in spelling*. London: Academic Press.

Bryant, P.E. & Bradley, L. (1983). Psychological strategies and the development of reading and writing. In M. Martlew (Ed.). *The psychology of written language: Developmental and educational perspectives*, (pp. 163–178). Chichester: Wiley.

Bryant, P.E. & Bradley, L. (1985). *Children's reading problems* Oxford: Blackwell.

Bryant, P.E., & Goswami, U. (1986). The strengths and weaknesses of the reading level design: comment on Backman, Mamen and Ferguson. *Psychological Bulletin*, *100*, 101–103.

Bryant, P.E. & Goswami, U. (1987). Phonological awareness and learning to read. In J. Beech and A. Colley (Eds), *Cognitive approaches to reading* (pp. 213–243). Chichester: Wiley.

Bryant, P.E. & Impey, L. (1986). The similarities between normal children and dyslexic adults and children. *Cognition*, *24*, 121–137.

Bryant, P.E., Bradley, L., MacLean, M. & Crossland, J. (1989). Nursery rhymes, phonological skills and reading. *Journal of Child Language*, *16*, 407–428.

Bryant, P.E., MacLean, M. & Bradley, L. (in press). Rhyme, language and children's reading. *Applied Psycholinguistics*.

Bryant, P.E., MacLean, M., Bradley, L. & Crossland, J. (in press). Rhyme and alliteration, phoneme detection and learning to read. *Developmental Psychology*.

Byrne, B. & Ledez, J. (1983). Phonological awareness in reading-disabled adults. *Australian Journal of Psychology, 35*, 185–197.

Calfee, R.C. (1977). Assessment of individual reading skills: basic research and practical applications. In A.S. Reber and D.L. Scarborough (Eds), *Toward a psychology of reading*. New York: Lawrence Erlbaum Associates Inc.

Calfee, R.C., Lindamood, P. & Lindamood, C. (1973). Acoustic-phonetic skills and reading: kindergarten through twelfth grade. *Journal of Educational Psychology, 64*, 293–298.

Campbell, R. (1985). When children write nonwords to dictation. *Journal of Experimental Child Psychology, 40*, 133–151.

Chukovsky, K. (1963). *From two to five*. Berkeley: University of California Press.

Coltheart, M. (1978). Lexical access in simple reading tasks. In G. Underwood (Ed.) *Strategies of information processing*. London: Academic Press.

Coltheart, M., Masterson J., Byng S., Prior M. & Riddoch J. (1983). Surface dyslexia. *Quarterly Journal of Experimental Psychology, 35*, 469–595.

Coltheart, V., Laxon, M.J., Keating, G.C. & Pool, M.M. (1986). Direct access and phonological encoding processes in children's reading: Effects of word characteristics. *British Journal of Educational Psychology, 56*, 255–270.

Conrad, R. (1964). Acoustic confusions in immediate memory. *British Journal of Psychology, 55*, 75–84.

Conrad, R. (1971). The chronology of the development of covert speech in children. *Developmental Psychology, 5*, 398–505.

Content, A., Morais, J., Alegria, J. & Bertelson, P. (1982). Accelerating the development of phonetic segmentation skills in kindergarteners. *Cahiers de Psychologie Cognitive, 2*, 259–269.

Content, A., Kolinsky R., Morais J. & Bertelson P. (1986). Phonetic segmentation in pre-readers: Effect of corrective information. *Journal of Experimental Child Psychology, 42*, 49–72.

Cossu, G., Shankweiler, D., Liberman, I.Y., Tola, G. & Katz, L. (1987). Awareness of phonological segments and reading ability in Italian children. *Haskins Labs Status Report on Speech Research*, No. SR–91.

Cunningham, A.E. (1988). *A developmental study of instruction in phonemic awareness*. Paper presented at the annual meeting of the American Educational Research Association, New Orleans, April 1988.

Doctor, E.A. & Coltheart, M. (1980). Children's use of phonological encoding when reading for meaning. *Memory and Cognition, 8*, 195–209.

Doctor, E.A., Antoine, W. & Scholnick, J. (1989). *Ambiguous phoneme-grapheme correspondence and its effect on children's spelling*. Paper presented at the International Conference on Cognitive Neuropsychology, Harrogate, England, July 1989.

Dodd, B. (1980). The spelling abilities of profoundly pre-lingually deaf children. In U. Frith (Ed.), *Cognitive processes in spelling* (pp. 423–540). London: Academic Press.

Dowker, A. (1989). Rhymes and alliteration in poems elicited from young children. *Journal of Child Language, 16*, 181–202.

Ehri, L.C. & Wilce, L.S. (1980). The influence of orthography on readers' conceptualisation of the phonemic structure of words. *Applied Psycholinguistics, 1*, 371–385.

Ellis, N.C. & Large, B. (1987). The development of reading: As you seek so shall you find. *British Journal of Developmental Psychology, 78*, 1–28.

Farnham-Diggory, S. & Simon, H.A. (1975). Retention of visually presented information in children's spelling. *Memory and Cognition, 3*, 599–608.

Fox, B. & Routh, D.K. (1975). Analyzing spoken language into words, syllables and phonemes: A developmental study. *Journal of Psycholinguistic Research, 4*, 331–342.

Frith, U. (1980). Unexpected spelling problems. In U. Frith (Ed.), *Cognitive processes in spelling*. London: Academic Press.

Frith, U. (1985). Beneath the surface of developmental dyslexia. In K. Patterson, M. Coltheart and J. Marshall (Eds), *Surface dyslexia*. London: Lawrence Erlbaum Associates Ltd.

Frith, U. & Snowling, M. (1983). Reading for meaning and reading for sound in autistic and dyslexic children. *British Journal of Developmental Psychology, 1*, 329–342.

Fuson, K.C. (1988). *Children's counting and concepts of number*. New York: Springer.

Gates, A.I. & Chase, E.H. (1926). Methods and theories of learning to spell tested by studies of deaf children. *Journal of Educational Psychology, 17*, 289–300.

Gelb, I.J. (1963). *A study of writing*. Chicago: University of Chicago Press.

Goswami, U. (1986). Children's use of analogy in learning to read: A developmental study. *Journal of Experimental Child Psychology, 42*, 73–83.

Goswami, U. (1988a). Orthographic analogies and reading development. *Quarterly Journal of Experimental Psychology, 40A*, 239–268.

Goswami, U. (1988b). Children's use of analogy in learning to spell. *British Journal of Developmental Psychology, 6*, 21–33.

Goswami, U. (1990a). Phonological priming and orthographic analogies in reading. *Journal of Experimental Child Psychology, 49*, 323–340.

Goswami, U. (1990b). A special link between rhyming skills and the use of orthographic analogies by beginning readers. *Journal of Child Psychology and Psychiatry, 31*, 301–311.

Guthrie, J.T. (1973). Reading comprehension and syntactic responses in good and poor readers. *Journal of Educational Psychology, 65*, 294–299.

Guthrie, J.T. & Seifert, M. (1977). Letter-sound complexity in learning to identify words. *Journal of Educational Psychology, 69*, 686–696.

Hall, J.W., Ewing, A., Tinzmann, M.B. & Wilson, K.P. (1981). Phonetic coding and dyslexic readers. *Bulletin of the Psychonomic Society 17*, 177–178.

Henderson, L. & Chard, J. (1980). The reader's implicit knowledge of orthographic structure. In U. Frith (Ed.), *Cognitive processes in spelling*. London: Academic Press.

Holligan, C. & Johnston, R.S. (1988). The use of phonological information by good and poor readers in memory and reading tasks. *Memory and Cognition, 16*, 522–532.

Johnston, R.S. (1982). Phonological coding in dyslexic readers. *British Journal of Psychology, 73*, 455–560.

Johnston, R.S., Rugg, M.D. & Scott, T. (1987). Phonological similarity effects, memory span and developmental reading disorders: The nature of the relationship. *British Journal of Psychology, 78*, 205–211.

Kimura, Y. & Bryant, P.E. (1983). Reading and writing in English and Japanese. *British Journal of Developmental Psychology, 1*, 129–144.

Kirtley, C., Bryant, P., MacLean, M. & Bradley, L. (1989). Rhyme, rime and the onset of reading. *Journal of Experimental Child Psychology, 48*, 224–245.

Kochnower, J., Richardson, E. & DiBenedetto, B. (1983). A comparison of phonic decoding ability of normal and learning disabled children. *Journal of Learning Disabilities, 16,* 348–351.

Lenel, J.C. & Cantor, J.H. (1981). Rhyme recognition and phonemic perception in young children. *Journal of Psycholinguistic Research, 10,* 57–68.

Liberman, I.Y., Shankweiler, D., Fischer, F.W. & Carter, B. (1974). Explicit syllable and phoneme segmentation in the young child. *Journal of Experimental Child Psychology, 18,* 201–12.

Liberman, I.Y., Shankweiler, D., Liberman, A.M., Fowler, C. & Fischer, F.W. (1978). Phonetic segmentation and recoding in the beginning reader. In A.S. Reber and D.L. Scarborough (Eds), *Toward a psychology of reading*. New York: Lawrence Erlbaum Associates Inc.

Lundberg, I., Olofsson, A. & Wall, S. (1980). Reading and spelling skills in the first school years predicted from phonemic awareness skills in kindergarten. *Scandinavian Journal of Psychology, 21,* 159–173.

Lundberg, I., Frost, J. & Petersen, O. (1988). Effects of an extensive program for stimulating phonological awareness in preschool children. *Reading Research Quarterly, 23,* 263–284.

MacLean, M., Bryant, P.E. & Bradley, L. (1987). Rhymes, nursery rhymes and reading in early childhood. *Merrill-Palmer Quarterly, 33,* 255–282.

Mann, V.A. (1984). Longitudinal prediction and prevention of early reading difficulty. *Annals of Dyslexia, 34,* 117–136.

Mann, V.A. (1986). Phonological awareness: the role of reading experience. *Cognition, 24,* 65–92.

Mann, V.A., Liberman, I.Y. & Shankweiler D. (1980). Children's memory for words strings in relation to reading ability. *Memory and Cognition, 8,* 329–335.

Marsh, G. & Desberg, P. (1983). The development of strategies in the acquisition of symbolic skills. In D.R. Rogers and J.A. Sloboda (Eds), *The acquisition of symbolic skills* (pp. 149–154). New York: Plenum.

Marsh, G., Desberg, P. & Cooper, J. (1977). Developmental strategies in reading. *Journal of Reading Behaviour, 9,* 391–394

Marsh, G., Friedman, M.P., Welch, V. & Desberg, P. (1980a). A cognitive-developmental approach to reading acquisition. In G.E. MacKinnon and T.G. Waller (Eds), *Reading research. Advances in theory and practice. Vol 3.* New York: Academic Press.

Marsh, G., Friedman, M.P., Welch, V. & Desberg, P. (1980b). The development of strategies in spelling. In U. Frith (Ed.), *Cognitive processes in spelling*. London: Academic Press.

Marsh, G., Friedman, M.P., Desberg, P. & Saterdahl, K. (1981). Comparison of reading and spelling strategies in normal and reading disabled children. In M.P. Friedman, J.P. Das and N. O'Connor (Eds), *Intelligence and learning* (pp. 363–367). New York: Plenum.

Marshall, J.C. (1984). Towards a rational taxonomy of developmental dyslexia. In R.N. Malatesha and H.A. Whitaker (Eds), *Dyslexia: A global issue*. The Hague: Nijhoff.

Marshall, J.C. & Newcombe, F. (1973). Patterns of paralexia: A psycholinguistic approach. *Journal of Psycholinguistic Research, 2,* 175–199.

Mitterer, J.O. (1982). There are at least two kinds of poor readers: whole word poor readers and recoding poor readers. *Canadian Journal of Psychology, 36,* 445–561.

Morais, J., Cary, L., Alegria, J. & Bertelson, P. (1979). Does awareness of speech as a sequence of phones arise spontaneously? *Cognition, 7,* 323–331.

Morais, J., Bertelson, P., Cary, L. & Alegria, J. (1986a). Literacy training and speech segmentation. *Cognition, 24,* 45–64.

Morais, J., Cluytens, M., Alegria, J. & Content, A. (1986b). Speech-mediated retention in dyslexics. *Perceptual and Motor Skills, 62,* 119–126.

Morais, J., Content, A., Bertelson, P., Cary, L. & Kolinsky, R. (1988). Is there a critical period for the acquisition of segmental analysis? *Cognitive Neuropsychology, 5,* 347–352.

Olson, R.K., Davidson, B.J., Kliegl, R. & Foltz, G. (1985). Individual and developmental differences in reading disability. In G.E. MacKinnon and T.G. Waller (Eds), *Reading Research: Advances in Theory and Practice, Vol. 4,* pp.1–64. New York: Academic Press.

Olson, R.K., Wise, B.W., Connors, F. & Rack, J. (in press). Organisation, heritability, & remediation of component word recognition and language skills in disabled readers. In T.H. Carr and B.A. Levy (Eds), *Reading and its development: Component skills approaches.* New York: Academic Press.

Patterson, K. & Morton, J. (1985). From orthography to phonology: An attempt at an old interpretation. In K.E. Patterson, J.C. Marshall and M. Coltheart (Eds), *Surface dyslexia* (pp. 335–360). London: Lawrence Erlbaum Associates Ltd.

Perfetti, C.A. (1985). *Reading ability.* Oxford: Oxford University Press.

Perfetti, C.A., Beck, I., Bell, L.C. & Hughes, C. (1987). Phonemic knowledge and learning to read are reciprocal: A longitudinal study of first grade children. *Merrill-Palmer Quarterly, 33,* 283–219.

Perin, D. (1983). Phonemic segmentation and spelling. *British Journal of Psychology, 74,* 129–144.

Piaget, J. (1952). *The child's conception of number.* London: Routledge and Kegan Paul.

Piaget, J. (1978). *The grasp of consciousness.* London: Routledge Kegan Paul.

Piaget, J. & Inhelder, B. (1958). *The growth of logical thinking from childhood to adolescence.* New York: Basic Books.

Pick, A., Unze, M., Brownell, C.A., Drozdal, J.G. & Hopmann, M.K. (1978). Young children's knowledge of word structure. *Child Development, 49,* 669–680.

Rack, J. (1989). *Reading-I.Q. discrepancies and the phonological deficit in reading disability.* Paper presented at the Biennial Meeting of the Society for Research in Child Development, Kansas City, MO, April 1989.

Read, C. (1971). Pre–school children's knowledge of English phonology. *Harvard Educational Review, 41,* 1–34.

Read, C. (1975). *Children's categorisations of speech sounds in English.* Urbana, Ill.: National Council of Teachers of English.

Read, C. (1986). *Children's creative spelling.* London: Routledge and Kegan Paul.

Read, C., Zhang, Y., Nie, H. & Ding, B. (1986). The ability to manipulate speech sounds depends on knowing alphabetic spelling. *Cognition, 24,* 31–44.

Reitsma, P. (1984). Sound priming in beginning reading. *Child Development, 55,* 406–523.

Rohl, M. & Tunmer, W.E. (1988). Phonemic segmentation skill and spelling acquisition. *Applied Psycholinguistics, 9,* 335–350.

Rosner, J. & Simon, D.P. (1971). *The auditory analysis test: an initial report.* Learning Research and Development Center, University of Pittsburgh.

Rozin, P., Bressman, B., & Taft, M. (1974). Do children understand the basic relationship between speech and writing? The mow-motorcyle test. *Journal of Reading Behaviour, 6,* 327–334.

Schlapp, U. & Underwood, G. (1988). Reading, spelling and two types of irregularity in word recognition. *Journal of Research in Reading, 11* 120–132.

Schonell, F. & Goodacre, E. (1971). *The psychology and teaching of reading*. 5th ed. London & Edinburgh: Oliver & Boyd.

Seymour, P.K. (1986). *Cognitive approaches to dyslexia*. London: Routledge Kegan Paul.

Seymour, P.K. & Elder, L. (1986). Beginning reading without phonology. *Cognitive Neuropsychology, 3*, 1–36.

Siegel, L.S. & Linder, B.A. (1984). Short term memory processes in children with reading and arithmetic learning disabilities. *Developmental Psychology, 20*, 200–207.

Siegel, L.S. & Ryan, E.B. (1988). Development of grammatical sensitivity, phonological, & short-term memory skills in normally achieving and learning disabled children. *Developmental Psychology, 24*, 28–37.

Share, D.L., Jorm, A.R., MacLean, R. & Matthews, R. (1984). Sources of individual differences in reading acquisition. *Journal of educational Psychology, 76*, 1309–1324.

Snowling, M.J. (1980). The development of grapheme-phoneme correspondence in normal and dyslexic readers. *Journal of Experimental Child Psychology, 29*, 294–305.

Snowling, M.J. & Frith, U. (1981). The use of sound, shape and orthographic cues in early reading. *British Journal of Psychology, 72*, 83–88.

Snowling, M.J., Stackhouse, J. & Rack J. (1986). Phonological dyslexia and dysgraphia—a developmental analysis. *Cognitive Neuropsychology, 3*, 309–339.

Stanovich, K.E., Cunningham, A.E. & Cramer, B.R. (1984). Assessing phonological awareness in kindergarten children: issues of task comparability. *Journal of Experimental Child Psychology, 38*, 175–190.

Stanovich, K.E., Nathan, R.G. & Vala-Rossi, M. (1986). Developmental changes in the cognitive co-ordinates of reading ability and the developmental lag hypothesis. *Reading Research Quarterly, 21*, 199–202.

Stanovich, K.E., Nathan, R.G. & Zolman, J.E. (1988). The developmental lag hypothesis in reading: Longitudinal and matched reading level comparisons. *Child Development, 59*, 71–86.

Stuart, M. & Coltheart, M. (1988). Does reading develop in a sequence of stages? *Cognition, 30*, 139–181.

Szeszulski, P.A. & Manis, F.R. (1987). A comparison of word recognition processes in dyslexic and normal readers at two reading age levels. *Journal of Experimental Child Psychology, 44*, 364–376.

Temple, C. (1986). Developmental dysgraphias. *Quarterly Journal of Experimental Psychology, 38A*, 77–110.

Temple, C. & Marshall, J.C. (1983). A case study of developmental phonological dyslexia. *British Journal of Psychology, 74*, 517–533.

Treiman, R. (1983). The structure of spoken syllables: Evidence from novel word games. *Cognition, 15*, 49–74.

Treiman, R. (1984). Individual differences among children in reading and spelling styles. *Journal of Experimental Child Psychology, 37*, 463–577.

Treiman, R. (1985a). Onsets and rimes as units of spoken syllables: evidence from children. *Journal of Experimental Child Psychology, 39*, 161–81.

Treiman, R. (1985b). Phonemic awareness and spelling: Children's judgements do not always agree with adults. *Journal of Experimental Child Psychology, 39*, 182–201.

Treiman, R. & Baron, J. (1981). Segmental analysis: development and relation to reading ability. In G.C. MacKinnon and T.G.Waller (Eds), *Reading research: Advances in theory and practice ,Vol III*. New York: Academic Press.

Treiman, R. & Hirsh-Pasek, K. (1985). Are there qualitative differences between dyslexic and normal readers? *Memory and Cognition, 13*, 357–364.

Tunmer, W.E. & Nesdale, A.R. (1985). Phonemic segmentation skill and beginning reading. *Journal of Educational Psychology, 77*, 417–527.

Tunmer, W.E., Nesdale, A.R. & Wright, A.D. (1987). Syntactic awareness and reading acquisition. *British Journal of Developmental Psychology, 5*, 25–34.

Tunmer, W.E., Herriman, M.L. & Nesdale, A.R. (1988). Metalinguistic abilities and beginning reading. *Reading Research Quarterly, 23*, 134–158.

Vellutino, F.R. (1979). *Dyslexia*. Cambridge, MA: MIT Press.

Wallach, M.A. & Wallach, L. (1976). *Teaching all children to read*. Chicago: University of Chicago Press.

Waters, G., Bruck, M. & Seidenberg, M.S. (1985). Do children use similar processes to read and spell words? *Journal of Experimental Psychology, 39*, 511–530.

Williams, J. (1980). Teaching decoding with an emphasis on phoneme analysis and phoneme blending. *Journal of Educational Psychology, 72*, 1–15.

Wimmer, H. (in press). A premature refutation of the logographic stage assumption: a critical comment on Stuart and Coltheart (1988). *British Journal of Developmental Psychology*.

Wimmer, H. & Hummer, P. (1989). *Does reading have to begin with a logographic stage: Negative evidence from German-speaking children*. Unpublished paper, Institut für Psychologie, University of Salzburg.

Wise, B.W., Olson, R.K. & Treiman, R. (1990). Subsyllabic units as aids in beginning readers' word learning: Onset-rime versus post-vowel segmentation. *Journal of Experimental Child Psychology, 49*, 1–19.

Yopp, H.K. (1988). The validity and reliability of phonemic awareness tests. *Reading Research Quarterly, 23*, 159–177.

Author Index

Subject Index